## Advance Praise for *Syntropy*

"The ICRL Press takes great satisfaction in offering this provocative treatise by Ulisse Di Corpo and Antonella Vannini, fastidiously edited by Brenda Dunne, ICRL's Editor-in-Chief. The book presents, in a readily readable format, a rare review of the work of the celebrated Italian mathematician Luigi Fantappiè regarding the concept, interpretation, and implications of the complementary principle to physical entropy, which he named syntropy. Along the way, the authors skillfully touch on a blazing array of related issues, ranging from the Klein-Gordon relations of relativistic quantum mechanics and their advanced wave solutions, to issues in evolutionary theory.

"Presenting pertinent empirical data to support their thesis, they also discuss the relevance of syntropy to time and water, negentropy and information, determinism and free will, and a host of correlative matters rich in implications to be contemplated and explored. If you are now holding this remarkable book in hand, scan the Table of Contents and prepare to be fascinated by its sweeping coverage of an alternative conceptualization of human experience and the nature of reality."
—Robert G. Jahn, Dean Emeritus, School of Engineering and Applied Science, Princeton University

"For many years now, Ulisse Di Corpo and Antonella Vannini have been furthering the revolutionary ideas of the Italian mathematician Luigi Fantappiè who in the 1940s coined the term syntropy to indicate order-producing influences propagating from the future into the present; a concept complementary to the disorder-producing entropic influences that propagate from the past into the present.

"Their message is getting crisper and more convincing, as they bring ever more evidence in support of this theory. They also show evidence that feelings, in particular love, may in fact be the form in which non-specific information from the future manifests into the present. These ideas bring a welcome sense of purpose and meaning into our worldview, absent if only the disorganizing entropy exists.

This theory can form the centerpiece of a new worldview that allows the unification of science and spirituality into a new paradigm where our inner aspects, exemplified by our thoughts and feelings, can be unified with the physical aspects that alone are now granted reality by science."
— Federico Faggin, co-inventor of the microprocessor and president of the Federico and Elvia Faggin Foundation

"Rarely in one's professional life as a physician and scientist does a book come along that truly offers a new way of looking at life and the universe. Such a book is that of Ulisse Di Corpo and Antonella Vannini on syntropy. A physical function in opposition to entropy has been sought by scientists for hundreds of years, especially for explaining the existence of life. Here, based on the original work of the mathematician Luigi Fantappiè in the 1940s and recent experimental evidence on retrocausality, we have a credible and well fleshed-out presentation of the implications of such a function in the principle of syntropy. The authors are to be congratulated for their courage and dedication to science for this work."
—Richard A. Blasband, M.D., research director of the Center for Functional Research in Sausalito, California

"While they continue to elucidate the rational fabric of the universe, few scientists these days give much thought to the meaning of their theories. But their left-brain world is far from being the whole story. Thus the authors of this book take an enormous stride by expanding science to connect our rational world to our emotional world—which, after all, is what really matters to us. Who would have thought that there could be a science of love? And one just as precise and formally correct as the science most of us have been brought up with?"
—Roger Taylor, PhD., independent researcher on subtle energy, and formerly Reader in Immunology, University of Bristol

# *Syntropy*
# THE SPIRIT of LOVE

ULISSE DI CORPO & ANTONELLA VANNINI

**ICRL Press**
*Princeton, New Jersey*

**SYNTROPY: The Spirit of Love**
By Ulisse Di Corpo and Antonella Vannini

Copyright © 2015
by Ulisse Di Corpo and Antonella Vannini

ISBN: 978-1-936033-17-1

Cover photo: Antonella Vannini

All rights reserved, including the right to reproduce
this book or portions thereof in any form whatsoever.
For information address:
ICRL Press
211 N. Harrison St., Suite C
Princeton, NJ 08540-3530

ICRL Press

# Table of Contents

Introduction ....................................................... 7

**1** Luigi Fantappiè and the Concept ............. 9
  of Syntropy

**2** Time and Water ......................................... 13

**3** An Extension of Thermodynamics .......... 19

**4** Negentropy, Syntropy and Information ... 25

**5** Experimental Evidence ............................. 27

**6** Determinism and Free Will ...................... 37

**7** The Unconscious Mind and the .............. 43
  Autonomic Nervous System

**8** Superconscious Mind and the Attractor ... 49

**9** Mind/Matter Interaction ......................... 53

**10** Heart or Brain? .......................................... 61

**11** Love or Instinct? ....................................... 65

**12** The Heart-Brain Axis ............................... 69

**13** Vital Needs ................................................. 75

| 14 | The Theorem of Love ............................... 79 |
| 15 | The Mystery of Life .................................. 87 |
| 16 | The Limits of Evolutionary Theory .......... 93 |
| 17 | Converging Evolution ............................ 103 |
| 18 | Attractors ................................................ 113 |
| 19 | The Balancing Role of Entropy ............. 123 and Syntropy |
| 20 | Syntropy Activation ............................... 129 |
| 21 | The Dual Solution of the ....................... 131 Fundamental Equations of Physics |
| 22 | The Paradox of Non-Locality ................. 135 |
| 23 | Diverging and Converging Cycles .......... 139 |
| 24 | Scientific Theories .................................. 145 |
| 25 | Relational Science .................................. 149 |
| 26 | Concluding Observations ....................... 151 |

About the Authors ............................................ 157

# INTRODUCTION

Most of us are familiar with the concept of entropy. Based on the second law of thermodynamics, it is a dissipative process that is a measure of the amount of thermal energy in a physical system that cannot be used to do work, and indicates the degree of disorder or uncertainty in that system. For example, it predicts that when heat flows from a region of high temperature to a region of low temperature the hot region becomes cooler and the cold region becomes warmer over time. This process occurs spontaneously without the need for any extra external energy. When it occurs we say that the entropy of the system has increased. The entropy of an isolated system always increases as it loses information and becomes less ordered. Expressions such as "you can't unscramble an egg" or "you can't take the cream out of the coffee" indicate the irreversibility of such processes.

Entropy is unidirectional and always proceeds forward in time. It explains the activity of many physical phenomena but fails to account for many others where order appears to increase spontaneously, where complexity develops from simple systems, or where disordered atoms form molecules. One can find such examples in ecological systems, certain characteristics of water, quantum entanglement and non-locality, retrocausality, healing, evolution, and life itself.

In 1942 Luigi Fantappiè proposed a law symmetric with entropy, which he named *syntropy*. Syntropy produces a continuous increase in complexity through the action of "attractors" that emanate from the future and provide systems with their purpose and design. Rather than generating disorder via increasing differentiation, syntropy draws individuals and systems together based on their similarities. In a certain sense, syntropy can be regarded as the action of love, which Louis de Broglie described as "that force which directs all of our delights and all of our pursuits. Indissolubly linked with thought and action, love is their common mainspring and, hence, their common bond."[1]

---

1. De Broglie, L., (1962), "The Role of the Engineer in the Age of Science," *New Perspectives in Physics*, trans. AJ. Pomerans. NY: Basic Books, p.213.

# 1 Luigi Fantappiè and the Concept of Syntropy

Luigi Fantappiè (1901–1956) was considered one of the foremost mathematicians of the 20th century. He graduated at the age of 21 from the most exclusive Italian university, *"La Normale Di Pisa,"* with a dissertation on pure mathematics, and became a full professor at the age of 27. During his university years he was a roommate of Enrico Fermi, worked with Werner Heisenberg, exchanged correspondence with Richard Feynman, and in April 1950 was invited by J. Robert Oppenheimer to become a member of the exclusive Institute for Advanced Study in Princeton and work with Albert Einstein and other notable scholars.

In 1941, while working on the *d'Alembert operator*, a formula for obtaining solutions to the quantum mechanical wave equation that combine special relativity and quantum mechanics, Fantappiè realized that the forward-in-time solution (i.e. *retarded waves*) describes energy and matter that diverge and tend towards homogeneous and random distributions. For example, when heat radiates from a radiator it tends to spread out in the environment. Fantappiè showed that although the retarded wave solution is governed by the law of entropy, the backward-in-time solution (i.e. *advanced waves*) is governed by a symmetric law that Fantappiè named *syntropy* (from the Greek *syn* = converging, *tropos* = tendency). The forward-in-time solution describes energy that diverges from a cause in the past. The backward-in-time solution, on the other hand, describes energy that converges towards future causes (i.e. *attractors*).

The properties of the law of syntropy are energy concentration, an increase in differentiation and complexity, a reduction of entropy, the formation of structures, and an increase in order. These are also the main properties that biologists observe in living systems, but cannot be explained by the classical time-forward models. This realization led Fantappiè to formulate *The Unitary Theory of the Physical and Biological World*, first published in 1942. There he suggests that we live in a super-causal universe, governed both by causality and retrocausality, and that *life is caused by the future*.[2]

Nowadays it is common to imagine time flowing from the past to the future, but imagining that past, present and future coexist is counterintuitive. Einstein's relativity started a new description of reality that is symmetrical with respect to time: on one side energy propagates from the past to

---

2. Fantappiè, L. (1942), "Sull'interpretazione dei potenziali anticipati della meccanica ondulatoria e su un principio di finalità che ne discende," *Rend. Acc. D'Italia*, 1942, 4(7).

the future, on the other side it propagates backward in time from the future to the past. Einstein used the term *Übercausalität* (supercausality) to refer to this new model of causality, yet, he was well aware that extending the current scientific paradigm to include supercausality would reopen the age-old conflict between science and religion, since that balance is based on the fact that science is limited to the study of classical causality, whereas religion deals with ends and final causes.

# TIME AND WATER

The law of syntropy maintains that causality can travel backward in time. Although we are accustomed to the presumption that causes always precede their effects, the law of syntropy, which stems from special relativity, describes time as a dimension of space in a way that is totally different from our intuitive logic. It is therefore important to start this work examining the three types of time that Einstein's energy/momentum/mass equation predicts:

*1. Causal time* is experienced when the positive energy solution prevails. That is, when systems diverge (such as our model of an expanding universe) and are governed by the properties of the forward-in-time energy solution. In diverging systems entropy prevails, causes always precede effects, and time flows forward from the past to the future. No advanced effects are possible under such conditions, such as light waves moving backwards in time or radio signals being received before they are broadcasted.

*2. Retrocausal time* is experienced when the negative energy solution prevails. That is, when systems converge and are governed by the properties of the backward-in-time energy solution (i.e. black-holes). In converging systems retrocausality prevails, effects precede causes, and time flows backwards from the future to the past. In these systems no retarded effects are possible, which is the reason why no light is emitted by black holes.

*3. Supercausal time* characterizes systems in which diverging and converging forces are balanced, and where causality and retrocausality coexist and complement one another. In such systems past, present and future time is unitary.

This classification of time recalls the ancient Greek division in *Kronos*, *Kairos* and *Aion*. *Kronos* describes familiar sequential causal time, made of absolute moments that flow from the past to the future. *Kairos* refers to retrocausal time. According to Pythagoras, *kairos* was the basis of intuition, the ability to feel the future and to choose the most advantageous options. *Aion* depicts supercausal time, where past, present and future coexist.

The question naturally arises of how the properties of life ascend from the quantum level of matter to the macroscopic level, transforming inorganic matter into organic matter. In 1925 the physicist Wolfgang Pauli discovered hydrogen bonding in water molecules, whereby the hydrogen atoms in water molecules share an intermediate position between the sub-atomic (quantum) and molecular (macrocosm) levels and provide a bridge that allows energy to flow from the quantum to the macroscopic level. The hydrogen bridge distinguishes water from all other liquids, increasing its attractive forces (syntropy) that are much more powerful than the van der Waals forces that hold together other liquids. Consequently, the entropy/syntropy hypothesis suggests that life originates from water at the quantum level, since at this level syntropy is available, and that life structures rapidly develop into the macroscopic level, governed by the opposite law of entropy. In order to survive the destructive effects of entropy, life needs to acquire the cohesive properties of syntropy and the unique properties of water provide that mechanism.[3]

> 1. When water freezes it expands and becomes less dense. The molecules of other liquids concentrate when they are cooled, solidify, become more dense and heavy, and sink. With water exactly the opposite is observed.

---

3. Ball, P. (1999). *H$_2$O: A Biography of Water*, London: Phoenix.

2. In most liquids the process of solidification starts from the bottom, since hot molecules move towards the top and cold molecules towards the bottom. In water, however, exactly the opposite happens: water solidifies starting from the top.

3. Water has a heat capacity far greater than that of other liquids and can absorb large quantities of heat, which is then released slowly. As a result, the amount of heat necessary to raise the temperature of water is far greater than what it is needed for other liquids.

4. When compressed, cold water becomes more fluid; in other liquids, viscosity increases with pressure.

5. Friction among surfaces of solids is usually high, whereas with ice friction is low and as a result ice surfaces are slippery.

6. At close to freezing temperatures the surfaces of ice adhere when they come into contact. This is the mechanism that allows snow to compact in snow balls; it is impossible to produce balls of flour, sugar, or other solid materials if no water is used.

7. Compared to other liquids, the differential between melting and boiling

temperatures in water is very large. Water molecules have high cohesive properties that increase the temperature needed to transform water from liquid to gas.[4]

Water is not the only molecule with hydrogen bonds. Ammonia and fluoride also form hydrogen bonds and these molecules also show anomalous properties similar to water. Water, however, produces a higher number of hydrogen bonds and this determines the high cohesive properties that link molecules in wide dynamic labyrinths.[5] Other molecules that form hydrogen bonds do not reach the point of being able to build networks and broad structures in space. Hydrogen bonds impose structural constraints that are extremely unusual for a liquid. One example of this structural constraint is provided by crystals of snow. When water freezes, the hydrogen bond mechanism stops along with the flow of syntropy between the micro and the macrocosm, eventually resulting in the death of a living system. Hydrogen bonds make water essential for life and ultimately water is the source of life that provides living systems with syntropy. The centrality and

---

4. Vannini, A. and Di Corpo, U. (2011), "Extraterrestrial Life, Syntropy and Water," *Journal of Cosmology*, Retrieved from http://journalofcosmology.com/Life101.html#18.

5. Bennun, A. (2013), "Hydration shell dynamics of proteins and ions couple with the dissipative potential of H-bonds within water," *Syntropy* 2013 (2): 328–333.

importance of water in life was eloquently described in marine biologist Rachel Carson's 1951 groundbreaking book, *The Sea Around Us*,[6] which explains why water is so essential to the origin and evolution of any biological structure.

---

6. Carson, R. (1951). *The Sea Around Us*. Oxford University Press.

# 3. AN EXTENSION OF THERMODYNAMICS

During the nineteenth century, the study and description of heat lead to a new discipline: thermodynamics. This discipline, which can be traced back to the works of Boyle, Boltzmann, Clausius, and Carnot, addresses the behavior of energy, of which heat is a form. The study of the transformation of heat into work led to the discovery of three laws:

*1. The law of conservation of energy*, which states that energy cannot be created or destroyed, but only transformed.

*2. The law of entropy*, which states that energy always moves from a state of availability to a state of unavailability. When transforming energy (for example from heat to work) part is lost to the environment and entropy is a measure of the quantity of energy that is lost. When this lost energy is distributed in a uniform way, a state of equilibrium is reached and it is no longer possible to transform energy into work. Entropy measures how close a system is to this state of equilibrium.

*3. The law of heat death*, which states that dissipated energy cannot be recaptured and used again, and that the entropy of an isolated system (which cannot receive energy or information from outside) can only increase until a state of equilibrium is reached.

Entropy introduces into physics the idea of irreversible processes. It maintains that energy always moves from a state of high potential to a state of low potential, tending to a state of equilibrium. In this regard, Sir Arthur Eddington stated that "entropy is the arrow of time," in the sense that it forces physical events to move from the past to the future.[7] Our experience continually informs us about entropy and the irreversible process that leads to the dissipation of energy and heat death: we see people become old and die; we see a fire losing intensity and turning into cold ashes; and we see entropy increasing in the world through pollution, depleted energy, and desertification. The irreversibility of entropy entails a one-way movement from order to disorder. Entropy measures the evolution of a physical system, and it is always associated with an increasing level of disorder.

Yet life defies entropy since it becomes more complex over time through growth and reproduction;

---

7. Eddington, A. (1935). *New Pathways in Science*. Cambridge University Press.

it turns the disordered atoms of the physical universe into very highly ordered molecules. Living systems evolve towards increasing order, towards higher forms of organization, diversification and complexity, and can avoid the heat death associated with reaching a maximum level of entropy.

Scientists have long debated this paradox. Erwin Schrödinger, who made many important contributions to the development of quantum mechanics, responded to the question of what allows life to counter entropy by noting that

> It feeds on negative entropy. It is by avoiding the rapid decay into the inert state of "equilibrium" that an organism appears so enigmatic; so much so, that from the earliest times of human thought some special non-physical or supernatural force (vis viva, entelechy) was claimed to be operative in the organism, and in some quarters is still claimed.[8]

A similar conclusion was reached by Albert Szent-Györgyi:

> It is impossible to explain the qualities of organization and order of living systems starting from the entropic laws of the

---

8. Schrödinger, E. (1944). *What is Life?* Retrieved from http://whatislife.stanford.edu/LoCo_files/What-is-Life.pdf

macrocosm. This is one of the paradoxes of modern biology: the properties of living systems are opposed to the law of entropy that governs the macrocosm.[9]

Szent-Györgyi went on to suggest the existence of a law symmetric to entropy:

> A major difference between amoebas and humans is the increase of complexity that requires the existence of a mechanism that is able to counteract the law of entropy. In other words, there must be a force that is able to counter the universal tendency of matter towards chaos and energy towards dissipation. Life always shows a decrease in entropy and an increase in complexity, in direct conflict with the law of entropy.

While entropy is a universal law that leads to the dissolution of any form of organization, life demonstrates the existence of another law. The main problem, according to Szent-Györgyi, is that:

> We see a profound difference between organic and inorganic systems...as a scientist I cannot believe that the laws of physics become invalid as soon as you enter the

---

9. Szent-Györgyi, A. (1977), "Drive in Living Matter to Perfect Itself," *Synthesis* 1, Vol. 1, No. 1, 14–26.

living systems. The law of entropy does not govern living systems.

Similar considerations were contemplated by the French palaeontologist, philosopher, and Jesuit priest Pierre Teilhard de Chardin, who recognized the need for a law symmetrical to entropy. In his influential book *The Phenomenon of Man* he noted:

> Reduced to its essence, the problem of life can be expressed as follows: once we admit the two major Laws of Energy Conservation and of Entropy (to which physics is limited), how can we add, without contradictions, a third universal law (which is expressed by biology)… The situation is clarified when we consider at the basis of cosmology the existence of a second kind of entropy (or anti-entropy).[10]

But in their present form, the laws of thermodynamics cannot accommodate syntropy. In order to do so the laws would need to be expanded.[11]

Perhaps the key to resolving this problem lies in the stipulation that the law of entropy applies only to closed or isolated systems that do not

---

10. Teilhard de Chardin, P. (2008). *Il fenomeno umano*. Brescia: Queriniana.

11. Vannini, A. and Di Corpo, U. (2012), "The New Thermodynamics and Life," *Syntropy* 2012 (2): 33-46.

exchange information with their environments. Living systems, by definition, interact with their environments by a constant exchange of information. Syntropy describes the acquisition of information that is a critical part of this dynamic.

# 4 NEGENTROPY, SYNTROPY AND INFORMATION

As we proceed, we will be making frequent reference to the concept of *information*, but since the term can mean different things depending on the context in which it is used, it might be helpful at this point to clarify its use in the discussion of the entropy/syntropy theory. In the same year in which Fantappiè discovered the law of syntropy, the American physicist Robert Lindsay coined the term *negentropy*, a term that came to be associated with *information theory*, and was derived from a formula developed by physicist Léon Brillouin for the purpose of quantifying the propagation of electrical signals in a telegraphic wire. Brillouin found that the propagation of information was in close correlation with the inverse of entropy, and therefore concluded that entropy is a measure of a lack of information in a physical system and that the reduction of entropy produces an increase of information.

Negentropy is often mistaken for syntropy, which can easily lead to the erroneous conclusion that an increase in information always corresponds to an increase in syntropy. Negentropy is defined as the *opposite* of entropy, whereas syntropy is defined as the *complement* of entropy. This may seem like a minor distinction, but it is an important one. Syntropic information flows from the future, whereas negentropic information flows from the past. This small difference makes syntropy and negentropy two totally different concepts. While opposites preclude each other, complements are not mutually exclusive, but balance one another, and complementarity is a significant factor in the entropy/syntropy dynamic.

#  EXPERIMENTAL EVIDENCE

The law of syntropy implies the existence of retrocausality, yet experiments capable of demonstrating it in physics laboratories under controlled conditions can pose substantial problems. John Wheeler and Richard Feynman's *Absorber Theory*, also known as the Wheeler-Feynman time-symmetric theory, an interpretation of electrodynamics, claims that all time-reversal symmetries lead to predictions identical with those of conventional electrodynamics. For this reason it is impossible to distinguish between time-symmetric results and conventional results.[12] And in his transactional interpretations of quantum mechanics, physicist John Cramer states that:

> Nature, in a very subtle way, may be engaging in backward-in-time handshaking. But the use of this mechanism is not available to experimental investigators even at the microscopic level. The completed transaction erases all advanced effects, so

---

12. Wheeler, J.A. and Feynman, R.P. (1945), "Interaction with the Absorber as the Mechanism of Radiation," *Reviews of Modern Physics* 17 (2–3): 157–161.

that no advanced wave signaling is possible. The future can affect the past only very indirectly, by offering possibilities for transactions.[13]

Fantappiè himself failed to devise experiments that could test his retrocausal hypothesis. In his "Unitary Theory of the Physical and Biological World" he stated that "anticipated waves do not obey classical causation; therefore they cannot be studied with experiments which obey the classical experimental method."[14]

Seventy years later, the present authors formulated the following testable hypothesis: "If life is sustained by syntropy, the parameters of the autonomic nervous system that support vital functions should react in advance to stimuli." And indeed an impressive number of studies have now shown that the autonomic nervous system (as measured by skin conductance and heart rate) can react *before* a stimulus is shown.[15] Several experimental studies of this kind were conducted

---

13. Cramer, J.G. (1986), "The Transactional Interpretation of Quantum Mechanics," *Reviews of Modern Physics*, Vol. 58: 647–688.

14. Fantappiè, L. (1944), *Principi di una teoria unitary a del mondo fisico e biologico*. Roma: Humanitas Nova.

15. Libet, B. (1985), "Unconscious cerebral initiative and the role of conscious will in voluntary action," *The Behavioral and Brain Sciences* 8: 529–566.

by Dean Radin, Senior Scientist at the Institute of Noetic Sciences, who monitored heart rate, skin conductance, and fingertip blood volume in subjects who were shown a blank screen for five seconds, followed by a randomly selected calm or emotional picture for three seconds. Radin found significant differences in the autonomic parameters *preceding* the exposure to emotional pictures versus calm pictures.[16,17]

Experiments using heart rate (HR) measurements were conducted in order to explore Fantappiè's retrocausal hypothesis. (A detailed review of the experiments and the description of four experiments conducted by the authors can be found in the book *"Retrocausality: Experiments and Theory."*[18]) These trials were divided in 3 phases:

*1. Presentation phase:* 4 colors were presented one after the other on a computer screen, with each color shown for exactly 4 seconds. The subject was asked to look at the colors while his or her

---

16. Radin, D. (2013). *Supernormal: Science, Yoga, and the Evidence for Extraordinary Psychic Abilities.* New York: Deepak Chopra Books.

17. Radin, D.I. (1997), "Unconscious perception of future emotions: An experiment in presentiment," *Journal of Scientific Exploration,* 11(2): 163–180.

18. Vannini, A. and Di Corpo, U. (2011). *Retrocausality: Experiments and Theory,* Kindle Editions, ASIN: B005JIN51O. A brief video presentation is available at http://youtu.be/5lvwlt1oBbQ.

heart beat frequency was measured at fixed intervals of 1 second. Four measurements of the heart rate (HR) were saved for each color, one every second, and the presentation of the color was found to be perfectly synchronized with the HR measurement. When necessary, the synchronization was re-established by showing a white image before the presentation of the first color in phase 1.

2. *Choice phase:* an image with 4 color bars was shown and the subject was allowed to choose (using the computer mouse) the color that he thinks the computer will select.

3. *Target phase:* the computer randomly selected the target color and showed the selected color full-screen on the computer.

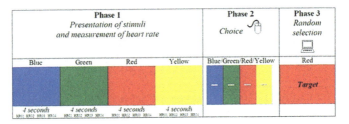

**Figure 1 – Experimental trials**

In the presence of Fantappiè's retrocausal effect, differences should be observed between HR measurements in phase 1 in concomitance to the color presented as the target color in phase 3. The presentation of the color in phase 3 was considered to be the cause of the HR differences observed in phase 1.

Trials were repeated 100 times per subject. Subjects were assisted only during the first trial and left alone for the remaining 99 trials. The first trial was therefore considered a test trial and not included in data analyses. In the following figure HR differences for one subject are graphically represented.

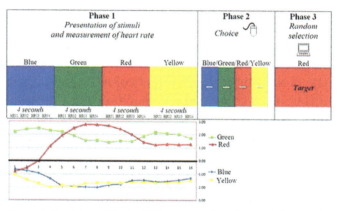

Figure 2 – Heart Rate differences in phase 1 for each target color selected in phase 3 (data from one subject)

Results showed that in phase 1 HR measurements associated with target colors differed from the base value. In the absence of a retrocausal effect, lines should vary around the base value (the 0.00 line). But results obtained comparing the average HR value of the 99 trials according to the target color selected in phase 3 differed significantly from the baseline.

The somatic markers (SM) hypothesis of Damasio and Bechara,[19] according to which emotions constitute a part of the decision making process instead of opposing it, found 3 types of autonomic nervous system responses:

1. after the gratification due to a gain;
2. after the punishment due to a loss;
3. before the subject decides what to choose.

Damasio interprets the anticipatory response as due to learning.[20] In order to compare Fantappiè's retrocausal hypothesis with Damasio's learning hypothesis, an experiment was devised in which the probability of each target color in phase 3 was different. A color had a 35% chance of being selected in phase 3 (lucky color) another had a 15% chance (unlucky color), and the remaining two colors each had a 25% probability. The task given to the subject was to guess the highest number of colors selected by the computer (target). Subjects were not aware that colors had a different chance of being selected. The three hypotheses of this experiment were as follows:

---

19. Bechara, A., Damasio, H., Tranel, D. and Damasio, A.R. (2005), "The Iowa Gambling Task and the somatic marker hypothesis: some questions and answers," *Trends in Cognitive Sciences*, vol. 9: 4, April 2005.

20. Damasio, A.R. (1994). *Descartes' Error. Emotion, Reason, and the Human Brain*, New York: Putnam.

*1. Retrocausal hypothesis:* statistically significant differences in heart rate measurements in phase 1 would be expected associated with targets (colors selected by the computer in phase 3). These differences would be interpreted as retrocausal effects, considering that the selection of target colors in phase 3 was totally unpredictable during phase 1.

*2. Learning hypothesis (classical causality):* according to Damasio and Bechara, a learning effect is expected in the form of heart rate differences in phase 1 in association with the choice (lucky and unlucky) operated by the subject in phase 2; these differences should increase during the conduct of the experiment.

*3. Interaction between retrocausal and learning effect (supercausality):* the retrocausal effect and the learning effect share similar somatic markers and are therefore both assessed through heart rates. The hypothesis is that at the beginning of the experiment only the retrocausal effect can be detected and then the learning effect would start to disturb the retrocausal effect which decreases, and at the end the retrocausal and learning effects separate and can be detected. Hints of a possible interaction between the learning and retrocausal effects emerged during the development of the experimental software. Subjects involved in previous experiments reported a "butterfly" feeling in the stomach in association with the choice of target stimuli, whereas subjects involved in testing the design of this last experiment did not report this feeling and the retrocausal effect was weaker. This suggested that the learning effect could disturb the retrocausal effect.

The results of this experiment showed a strong retrocausal effect on all colors, which was assessed as anticipatory reactions of HR in phase 1 according to the color shown by the computer in phase 3. This effect was observed beginning with the first trials, as predicted by the retrocausal hypothesis. The learning effect was assessed in the form of anticipatory reactions of HR in phase 1 according to the color chosen by the subject in phase 2. The learning effect emerged in the last block of trials of the experiment, as predicted by the learning hypothesis, according to which a learning effect requires time to build up. The interaction between the two effects was also assessed in the central part of the experiment in which the learning effect inhibits the retrocausal effect.

Several experiments were conducted in order to search for artifacts. For example, in one experiment the target was always selected in phase 3 by the computer, but it was randomly replaced with a gray color. The retrocausal effect appeared only when the target color was shown to the subject in phase 3, excluding in this way the possibility of forward-in-time processes that could affect the random selection of the color in phase 3.

The results of all these experiments were consistent with Fantappiè's retrocausal hypothesis, displaying heart rate measurements that correlated significantly with future stimuli.

# 6 DETERMINISM AND FREE WILL

Feelings that attract towards future aims act as a *pull factor* and provide motivations and direction, whereas information based on past experiences and knowledge acts as a *push factor* that is usually regarded as deterministic. Within a scientific perspective that rejects the possibility of backward causation, it is not surprising that most studies of consciousness tend approach the topic in a deterministic fashion. As a result, the prevailing assumption about the nature of mind is that it is the product of push factors emanating from brain activity.

Studying neurological patients affected by decision-making deficits, Antonio Damasio noted that the pull factor is not present in patients with specific lesions of the prefrontal cortex that integrate signals arriving from the body. These patients show an absence or imperfect perception of feelings and a behavior that can be described as "shortsighted toward the future."[21] Damasio suggested that feelings constitute an important part of

---

21. Damasio, A.R. (1994). *Descartes' Error. Emotion, Reason, and the Human Brain*, New York: Putnam.

the decision-making process, rather than opposing it, and help to promote advantageous choices without having to produce advantageous assessments.

The duality between past and future exists in our mind in the form of rational and intuitive thinking, and may be related to the specialization of the two cerebral hemispheres. The cortex is not a single block, but is split into the left hemisphere, postulated to be the seat of temporal and logical reasoning, and the right hemisphere, which appears to be nonlinear and associated with intuitions, global processing, analogies, symbols, and colors. The left hemisphere thus deals primarily with the external and material world, characterized by objective information and analytical rational thinking; the right hemisphere, on the other hand, deals more with our inner world, and is characterized by feelings, intuitive processes, images, and associations.

In Western culture, attention has become increasingly driven by the left-hemisphere processes: writing, quantification, diagrams, and other demonstrations of the physical world. We can now describe an object by its characteristics and use standardized symbols and mathematics to represent them, and we can attempt to reconstruct retrospectively the parts of a whole by analytical processes. We usually are not able to look at objects and ourselves, however, from the inside and experience the essence of reality and, generally speaking, we tend to overlook intuitions and feelings in the process of objectifying our experience. When only *push factors*, governed by the law of entropy, and not the *pull factors* governed by the law of syntropy, control our reality, it is easy to regard it as deterministic and forget that it is our dreams and feelings that draw us toward our goals. Some successful people maintain that they feel they came into the world for a purpose, or with an unconscious "blueprint," and that when they follow that purpose, even if intuitively, events leading to that purpose seem to unfold more easily.

Seen objectively, from the outside, events usually appear to be driven by deterministic forces from the past that are entropic in nature. When we are able to experience events subjectively from the inside, however, the same events seem to be more malleable and adaptable to our purposes. Which view we choose is an expression of free will.

A growing body of empirical evidence on the anticipatory reactions of the parameters of the autonomic nervous system, such as that discussed earlier, suggests that the activity of the autonomic nervous system must be included in any model of the mind. According to the entropy/syntropy theory, the autonomic nervous system connects the individual to the attractor, the source of our vital energy (syntropy), and it is therefore the seat of the *feeling of life*: the Self.

The entropy/syntropy theory posits that the mind is organized on three levels, the *conscious mind, the unconscious mind,* and the *superconscious mind.* The *conscious mind* to which we are tuned during the time we are awake, connects us to the physical level of reality. It mediates feelings that come from the autonomic nervous system, i.e. the unconscious mind, with information that comes from the physical world. The *unconscious mind* governs the involuntary vital functions of the body, such as heartbeat, digestion, regenerative functions, growth, development, and reproduction, and can be accessed through dreams, or via techniques of relaxation and altered states of consciousness such as hypnotic trance. It also implements highly automated programs that allow us to perform many complex tasks without having to think continuously about them, such as walking, riding a bicycle, driving, etc. The autonomic nervous system supplies the body with the properties of syntropy.

The *superconscious mind* is that part of our being that is directly associated with the attractor. The attractor is the source of syntropy (i.e. life energy) that provides purpose, mission, and meaning to our existence and receives the experiences of all the individuals who are connected to it, for example the members of the same species. It selects information that is advantageous for life and relays it to all the individuals, as well as serving as a natural memory bank that conserves the trace of all things in space and time, similar to the popular idea of the Akashic Field. The super-conscious mind shows the way, provides solutions and answers, and is the source of inspiration, providing knowledge and intelligence that allow us to solve problems. It can communicate with the conscious mind symbolically in dreams, or in the form of feelings of anticipation, presentiments, insights and inspirations.

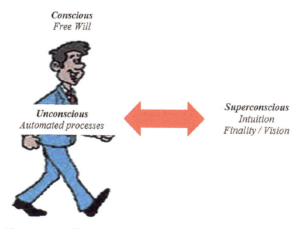

**Figure 3 – The conscious, unconscious and superconscious mind**

# 7. THE UNCONSCIOUS MIND AND THE AUTONOMIC NERVOUS SYSTEM

The autonomic nervous system is responsible for acquiring the properties of syntropy and distributing them in the form of life energy to the vital processes of the body that nourish regeneration and healing. It connects the individual with the attractor that gives shape, organization, and structure to the physical body. According to the entropy/syntropy theory, the design of living systems is contained in the attractor that retroacts from the future.

When we try to explain the complexity and order of genetic information solely as a result of past causes, we face a series of logical contradictions and paradoxes. In fact, since the processes of random genetic mutation are governed by the law of entropy, they can only lead to a gradual increase of the structural differences between individuals, thereby preventing the formation of species. In the real world, however, we witness just the opposite: namely an incredible convergence of biological structures that lend themselves towards common designs despite individual differences. For example, we can definitely indicate different races of human beings, such as Europeans, Asians, Africans, but there is something that unites all of these individuals and makes them all part of humanity. Considering only cause and effect relations, it is impossible to explain either the convergence of different individuals towards the same species, or the stability of species in time. The entropy/syntropy theory suggests that the design of a species is held in specific attractors that retroact from the future; attractors that connect individuals of the same species. An example of this process is provided by the experiments conducted by biologist Rupert Sheldrake, who showed that learning a task is shared (in an invisible and immaterial way) with all the other individuals who belong to the same species and not among individuals of different species. When a common attractor is shared in this way, the discoveries of one individual can be disseminated to all the other individuals of that species via the bridge (attractor) among its individuals. Sheldrake conducted a series of experiments that demonstrated that members of the same attractor, such as animals belonging to the same species, are able to share knowledge without any physical contact or any other way that might allow the sensory transmission of knowledge and information. These experiments were very simple: animals learned a new behavior that is advantageous for their survival, and other animals that belong to the same species showed a tendency to learn the same behavior more quickly.

The verb *to inform* derives from the Latin term *in-formare* that means to give a form. Aristotle claimed that information is a more truly primitive fundamental activity than energy and matter. Information does not have an immediate meaning, such as world knowledge, but rather it encompasses a modality that precedes every physical form. Once there is a form, the potential information can become expressed through one of its possible manifestations. The autonomic nervous system connects the individual to the attractor and provides information and syntropy to all the vital processes, including morphogenesis. These processes occur at the level of the unconscious mind, since they are vital and do not depend on free will despite the incredible amount of intelligence that they require.

The autonomic nervous system, i.e. the unconscious mind:

1. Is guided by feelings of anticipation that lead towards specific forms and solutions;

2. Provides syntropic vital energy to the various organs of the body and performs healing actions based on the designs received from the attractor;

3. Behaves like a mechanic who consults the manual of the manufacturer to perform repairs and maintain the system as close as possible to the

project. (Of course, the project is not mechanical and instructions are written with the ink of emotions);

4. Underlies all the involuntary functions of the body and it is responsible for controlling the motion of muscles and limbs;

5. Governs all the functions of the body that are not subject to choice and which do not require action on the conscious level. For example, it is responsible for digestion, heart rate, assimilation of food, and cell regeneration, all processes that are inaccessible to the conscious mind. We do not know how they are carried out, and often we do not even know that they exist. One need not be a doctor or a biologist in order to digest food or regenerate a tissue. The body knows all this independently, and shows an extraordinary level of innate intelligence;

6. Directs and regulates these processes, thereby expressing the capabilities and potentialities of an intelligence that is considerably more complex than the conscious mind;

7. Memorizes patterns of behavior, which it then executes autonomously and automatically, and which are maintained over time, giving rise to habits. This memory is then stored, at least in part, in the muscles of the body in the form of patterns of behavior;

8. Repeats behavioral patterns until they become habits that are activated automatically, independently of our will. These patterns are then placed firmly in the memory of the unconscious mind. The conscious mind often does not remember what was included in the memory of the unconscious mind. Consequently the unconscious mind can open incredible scenarios in the process of learning to know ourselves;

9. Also acts as a guardian of any information that the conscious mind cannot comfortably handle.

#  SUPERCONSCIOUS MIND AND THE ATTRACTOR

According to the entropy/syntropy model, the superconscious mind originates in the attractor, outside our physical being and connected to our body via the solar plexus (i.e. the heart). Since syntropy acts as an absorber and concentrator of energy, the strong functioning of the superconscious mind is associated with feelings of warmth located in the heart area, feelings that coincide with the experience of love. In contrast, weak functioning of the superconscious mind is associated with feelings of emptiness and emotional pain, anxiety and anguish, often accompanied by physical symptoms such as nausea, dizziness, and feelings of suffocation. The superconscious is a state that leads to a higher level of awareness and allows us to experience visions of the future, intuitions, and inspirations that are usually inaccessible to the ordinary states of the conscious mind. Each individual constantly interacts with the superconscious mind, which illuminates the direction, provides aims, and clarifies the mission of our life.[22] We connect with the superconscious mind in moments of silence and when we avoid activities and habits that distract us from our inner feelings. The superconscious mind is available to everyone, and acts as an inner teacher who guides us towards wellbeing and the solution of problems.

Henri Poincaré's description of intuition perhaps can help better to understand the role of the attractor:

> The genesis of mathematical creation is a problem which should intensely interest the psychologist. To invent is to choose; but the word is perhaps not wholly exact. In mathematics the samples would be so numerous that a whole lifetime would not suffice to examine them.[23]

Poincaré noticed that when faced with a new mathematical problem he began using the rational approach of the mind that allowed him to become aware of the characteristics and elements of the problem. But since the options tended to be infinite and it would take too much time

---

22. Aydin, A. (2010). *Human Drama – Struggle for Finding the Lost Spirit*, 7th Symposium on Personal and Spiritual Development in the World of Cultural Diversity. The International Institute for Advanced Studies (IIAS).

23. Poincaré, H. (1800), *Arch. Néerland. Sci.* 2, 5, 252–278.

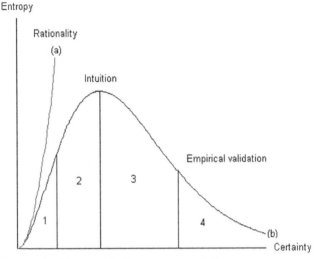

**Figure 4 - Phases of the process of discovery**

and intuitions, entropy increases, as is illustrated by line a.

A similar model has been developed by Sergio Barile in the "*Viable Systems Approach*"[24] using the term *abduction*, a term first introduced by the American philosopher Charles Sanders Peirce,[25] a form of logical inference that goes from observation to a hypothesis and seeks to explain relevant evidence.

---

24. Barile, S. (2009). *Management Sistemico Vitale*, Torino: Giappichelli Editore.

25. Peirce, C.S. (c. 1906). "Prolegomena to an Apology for Pragmatism," MS 293, *New Elements of Mathematics* v. 4, pp. 319–320.

to evaluate them all, some other type of process started operating that led him to the correct answer. He named this process *intuition* and considered it a process that is fundamental in the production of qualitatively new information. Poincaré came to the conclusion that the process of discovery can be divided into four phases:

1. A *conscious phase* that requires a period of work, during which we become aware of the elements that constitute the problem;

2. An *unconscious phase* in which intuitive processes take place and lead to the correct solution, which is highlighted by a feeling of warmth and wellbeing in the heart area, and a sense of *truth* that draws the attention of the mind;

3. A *phase of formalization*. What the unconscious presents to the conscious mind in the form of an intuition is not a final or complete argumentation, but rather a starting point from which we can work out the details.

4. A *phase of validation* in which the formalized concepts are translated into hypotheses and verified.

According to Poincaré, intuitions guide towards the right solutions and options, in this way reducing entropy (line b). To the contrary, when we use only rational thinking, neglecting the heart

# 9 MIND/MATTER INTERACTION

Descartes famously distinguished between two types of substance: *res extensa*, the so-called objective reality, and *res cogitans*, our conscious experience. In the introduction to *The Conscious Mind*, David Chalmers states that *"It still seems utterly mysterious that the causation of behavior should be accompanied by a subjective inner life,"*[26] and he divides the problems of consciousness into t*he easy problem*, which deals with the study of neurobiological models of consciousness and neural correlates of the conscious experiences, and t*he hard problem*, which deals with the subjective qualities of conscious experience, since these subjective aspects escape a materialistic analysis.

Chalmers affirms that easy problems are easy because all that it is needed is to find the mechanisms that explain them and make them compatible with the laws of classical physics. The hard problem of consciousness is difficult because even when all the main functions are explained according to cause-effect processes it is impossible

---
26. Chalmers, D. (1996). *The Conscious Mind: In Search of a Fundamental Theory*, Oxford University Press.

to arrive at the explanation of the subjective qualities of consciousness within the laws of classical physics.

The entropy/syntropy hypothesis solves the hard problem by showing that there is only one *"energy"* and that two forces apply to this: one diverging (i.e. *res extensa*), which propagates forward in time, and one converging (i.e. *res cogitans*), which propagates backward in time. When we expand physics to the negative-time solution of energy the hard problem is solved. This implies that in the mind/matter interaction both elements should always be at play. It also suggests that mind and matter continuously interact, producing effects that are considered anomalous according to the laws of classical physics.

The PEAR laboratory (*Princeton Engineering Anomalies Research*), founded in 1979 by Robert Jahn, then Dean of the School of Engineering and Applied Sciences of Princeton University, and Brenda Dunne, the PEAR laboratory manager, conducted extensive experiments over some 28 years to determine whether human consciousness could influence the behavior of a variety of random physical systems. A substantial component of these employed microelectronic random event generators or REGs, where human operators attempted to shift the means of the output distributions in a desired direction.

The history and results of the PEAR laboratory are described in detail in Jahn and Dunne's books *Margins of Reality: The Role of Consciousness in the Physical World,*[27] and *Consciousness and the Source of Reality: The PEAR Odyssey.*[28] In brief, over many tens of millions of trials performed on a variety of random physical devices by more than a hundred participants, none of whom claimed any exceptional abilities in this regard, the ability of human consciousness to introduce small, but significant, increments of order into these random processes was repeatedly demonstrated.

The following graph displays the cumulative results of over 2.5 million experimental trials, produced by 91 subjects over twelve years at the PEAR laboratory, indicating significant mean shifts that correlated with operators' *intentions*. The independent variable in all these trials was the intention of the subject to distort the REG distributions towards high or low mean values, or to produce a baseline with no stated intention.

---

27. Jahn, R.G. and Dunne, B.J. (2009). *Margins of Reality: The Role of Consciousness in the Physical World.* Princeton, NJ: ICRL Press, p.203. (Originally published by Harcourt Brace Jovanovich in 1987.)

28. Jahn, R.G. and Dunne, B.J. (2011). *Consciousness and the Source of Reality: The PEAR Odyssey.* Princeton, NJ: ICRL Press.

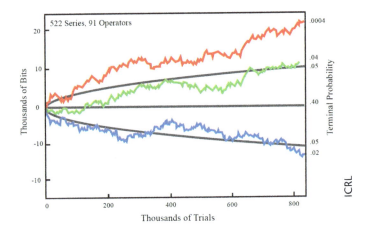

Figure 5 – Cumulative deviations from the Gaussian mean value

The PEAR group also conducted 396,000 trials in a remote version of the protocol, where the operator and the REG system were spatially separated by distances up to 5,000 miles. The REG system was started at agreed-upon times, but without the experimenters' knowledge of the subjects' intentions. The results were similar to those produced in the local protocol where the REG system and the subject shared the same room and the same moment in time. In an "off-time" variation of this experiment, the REG system was activated either many hours, or even days, *before* or *after* the expression of the operators' intentions. The different modalities of local, remote, on time, and off-time are shown in the following figure and indicate a significant increase in the size of the effect in the off-time/retrocausal modality. All told, some 30 subjects generated over 1.5 million trials in the remote and off-time experiments.

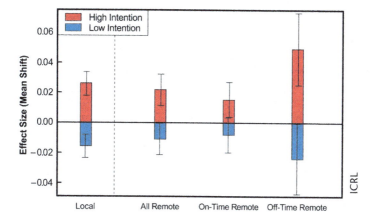

Figure 6 – Comparisons between local and remote experiments, and between on-time and off-time protocols. (The height of the bars show the mean values of the trials, with indications of the probabilities beyond which values become statistically significant.)

Another variation of the PEAR REG experiments with direct relevance for the syntropy hypothesis involved a body of data produced by two operators working together with a shared intention. These were termed "Co-Operator" studies, and results showed effects that were on average twice as strong as those produced by the same individuals working alone, *as long as they were of opposite sex*. The output of *same-sex* pairs showed no effects beyond chance, even if the participants previously had been individually successful. If the opposite-sex co-operators were emotionally bonded couples, however, their average effects were nearly seven times larger than their individual results. Figure 9 compares the results for the same- and opposite-sex pairs.

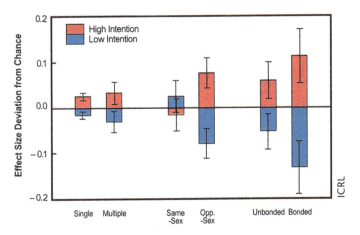

**Figure 7** – Block graph display of effect sizes for various categories of co-operator results (1σ error bars superimposed)[29,30]

Operator gender was also found to be a significant factor across all the PEAR experiments, with males and females typically producing distinctly different overall patterns of results. The male

---

29. Dunne, B.J. (1991). "Co-Operator Experiments with an REG Device." PEAR Technical Report *#91005*.

30. Jahn, R.G. and Dunne, B.J. (2011). *Consciousness and the Source of Reality: The PEAR Odyssey*. Princeton, NJ: ICRL Press.

operators tended to produce small effects that were correlated with their intentions, while the females generated larger effects, but both their high and low efforts were in the high direction, but to a degree that exceeded chance in both conditions. Even the baselines, or control conditions, where no stated intention was involved, displayed anomalous gender-specific shifts of the distribution means. The males' baselines showed reduced variances and means that remained very close to chance. The females' baselines, on the other hand, tended to display large variances and means that departed significantly from chance.

The fact that these gender-related effects appear to be amplified when produced by a resonant loving couple may be telling us something important about the capacity of love to introduce order into otherwise random processes. The findings of these rigorously controlled laboratory experiments thus support the two key elements at play in the entropy/syntropy model of the mind: conscious intention and emotions/feelings, and display strong evidence of retrocausality.

In their publications *"FieldREG Anomalies in Group Situations"*[31] and *"FieldREG II: Consciousness*

---

31. Nelson, R.D, Bradish, J.G., Dobyns, Y.H., Dunne, B.J, and Jahn, R.G. (1996), "FieldREG Anomalies in Group Situations," *Journal of Scientific Exploration*, 10, No.1, pp.111–141.

*Field Effects: Replications and Explorations"*[32] the PEAR group describe another body of REG experiments conducted in different environments. These experiments, named *FieldREG*, showed that the mind/machine interaction can be enhanced in emotionally "resonant" group environments, whereas the effects diminished when the experiment was conducted in mundane or "non-resonant" settings. The differences observed between the resonant and non-resonant settings show a statistical significance with odds of 3 in 100 million that the effects were not due to chance, and again demonstrate that shared emotions play an important role in anomalous mind/machine interactions.

The PEAR group also conducted many hundreds of experiments in a phenomenon they called *remote perception* (also known as *remote viewing*). Extensive statistical analyses confirmed beyond any possible doubt that people are able to obtain viable information about geographical locations over global distances, up to many days *before* or *after* the location was identified.[33]

---

32. Nelson, R.D., Jahn, R.G., Dunne, B.J., Dobyns, Y.H., and Bradish, J.G. (1998), "FieldREGII: Consciousness Field Effects: Replications and Explorations,"*Journal of Scientific Exploration*, 12, No.3, pp. 425–454.

33. Dunne, B.J. and Jahn, R.G. (2003), "Information and Uncertainty in Remote Perception Research," *Journal of Scientific Exploration*, 17 (2) pp. 207–241.

# 10 HEART OR BRAIN?

One of the main differences between the model of the mind that emerges from the entropy/syntropy theory and other models in the scientific literature is that the syntropic model of the mind is heart-centered, whereas most other models of the mind and consciousness are typically brain-centered.

According to the prevailing brain-driven model, consciousness is produced by the brain, and when the brain stops working the person is regarded as dead. In 2008, when the Vatican declared that brain death cannot be used to determine the end of a life, the Western medical/scientific world responded by claiming that: "The criteria for brain death is the only scientifically valid criteria in order to sanction the death of an individual," and that, moreover, "the criticism that comes from fringe minority, are based essentially on non-scientific considerations."[34]

Rita Levi-Montalcini (1909–2012), Italian neurobiologist who, together with colleague Stanley

---

34. De Mattei, R. (2005). *Finis Vitae*. Città del Vaticano: Rubbettino.

Cohen, received the 1986 Nobel Prize in Physiology for their discovery of nerve growth factor (NGF), reconsiders the centrality of the brain:

> Everyone says that the brain is the most complex organ of the body. As a doctor I might agree! But as a woman, I assure you that there is nothing more complex than the heart; its mechanisms are still unknown. In the brain there is logical reasoning, in the reasoning of the heart there are "emotions."[35]

The entropy/syntropy theory maintains that life and consciousness are sustained by the backward-in-time flow of energy (syntropy), which is absorbed by the autonomic nervous system, and that the feeling of life is most likely in the heart, rather than the brain.

Heart or Brain? This is one of the main differences between the philosophies of the West and the East. The West is brain-centered, whereas Asia, and especially China, is heart-centered. An example is provided by the term "heart" itself. The Chinese ideogram for heart translates to: bosom, center, core, feeling, thinking and intelligence. These are some of the main properties of what in the West we call consciousness. Yet we

---

35. Retrieved from http://en.alessandrodelpiero.com/news/happy-womens-day_340.html.

associate consciousness with the brain, while Chinese ideograms invariably associate consciousness to the heart and suggest that when it comes to consciousness, the emphasis should shift from the head to the heart. This same emphasis can be found in the traditions of many other early civilizations. In ancient Egypt, for example, the heart was considered to be the seat of consciousness, whereas the brain was considered unnecessary fat material. In ancient Greek, Roman, Indian, Arab, and Jewish cultures the scientific, medical, philosophical, and mystical systems also considered the heart the seat of consciousness, with the brain a tool subject to the dictates of the heart.

# 11 LOVE OR INSTINCT?

In China the ideogram for love, 春心, is expressed by the combination of the ideograms 春 (life) and 心 (heart), whereas in the West love is attributed to the action of neurotransmitters and regarded as a manifestation of reproductive instinct. Subjective concepts like love are not recognized in the West as being necessary for the survival and reproduction of the species since they can be explained by neurophysiological processes. For example, a recent paper by two British anthropologists, Robin Dunbar and Anna Maschin[36] claimed that the need for friendship can easily be explained as being produced by internal opioids (endorphins) that are generated during friendship relations. Friendship is a scientific paradox, therefore, and it remains a mystery why we spend enjoyable hours with people from whom we will probably never receive any survival benefit. For this reason, Dunbar and Maschin state that since friendship is caused by an internal drug it has the same addictive effects of psychotropic drugs.

---

36. Maschin, A.J. and Dunbar, R.I.M. (2011), "The brain opioid theory of social attachment: a review of the evidence," *Behaviour*, 148(10): 985–1025.

Endogenous opioids (or endorphins) are neurotransmitters associated with a state of wellness, which encourage us to see life optimistically and reduce stress hormones. According to mainstream science, these endorphins are the cause of wellbeing and, as Dunbar and Maschin put it, they "are the glue that makes us keep those neurochemical complex social relationships that go beyond mating and care of offspring."

The entropy/syntropy theory reverses this interpretation, arguing that love, friendship, and emotional resonance are vital expressions of our need to acquire syntropy. Syntropy is cohesive and convergent and its manifestations are expressions of union and feeling of connectedness. When we acquire syntropy, we experience feelings of warmth due to the concentration of life energy, and feelings of wellbeing caused by the regenerative processes activated by life energy. Obviously, these processes produce endorphins, but their production is regarded as a consequence rather than a cause.

Fantappiè was impressed by the fact that he could see the law of love in the fundamental equations of the universe:

> Today we see printed in the great book of nature—that Galileo said, is written in mathematical characters—the same law

of love that is found in the sacred texts of major religions.[37]

He described this finding in the following way:

> What makes life different is the presence of syntropic qualities: finalities, goals, and attractors. Now as we consider causality the essence of the entropic world, it is natural to consider finality the essence of the syntropic world. It is therefore possible to say that the essence of life is the final causes, the attractors. Living means tending to attractors… the law of life is not the law of mechanical causes; this is the law of nonlife, the law of death, the law of entropy; the law which dominates life is the law of finalities, the law of syntropy. But how are these attractors experienced in human life? When a man is attracted by money we say he loves money. The attraction towards a goal is felt as love. We now see that the fundamental law of life is this: the law of love. I am not trying to be sentimental; I am just describing results which have been logically deducted from premises which are sure. It is incredible and touching that, having arrived at this point, mathematical theorems start speaking to our heart!

---

37. Fantappiè, L. (1955). *Conferenze scelte*. Roma: Di Renzo Editore.

The law of life is not the law of hate, the law of force, or the law of mechanical causes; this is the law of non-life, the law of death, the law of entropy. The law which dominates life is the law of cooperation towards goals which are always higher, and this is true also for the lowest forms of life. In humans this law takes the form of love, since for humans living means loving, and it is important to note that these scientific results can have great consequences at all levels, particularly on the social level, which is now so confused.... The law of life is therefore the law of love and differentiation. It does not move towards leveling and conforming, but towards higher forms of differentiation. Each living being, whether modest or famous, has its mission, its finalities, which, in the general economy of the universe, are important, great and beautiful.

# 12 THE HEART-BRAIN AXIS

For a long time the heart has been considered simply as a mechanical pump that provides the propulsion of blood in the circulatory system. Professor Carlo Ventura, at the Laboratory of Cardiovascular Sciences of the National Institutes of Health in Baltimore, started to investigate the possibility that the cardiac tissue could be the target of the action of endorphins, small proteins that were believed to act only at the central nervous system level in order to adjust the perception of pain and other cognitive functions.[38] The idea that these proteins might be involved in the regulation of the cardiovascular system came from the finding of elevated levels of endorphins in patients with heart attack, suffering from a severe failure of the contraction of the heart.

During experiments, the presence of specific receptors that can bind endorphins and trigger profound changes in calcium levels and contractility of the heart were found. These studies, conducted in the early nineties, show that the brain is not

---

38. Ventura, C. (2003), Zinellu, E., Maninchedda, E., Fadda, M., Maioli, M., "Protein kinase C signaling transduces endorphin-primed cardiogenesis in GTR1 embryonic stem cells," *Circ. Res.*, online supplement, 92, 1–20.

the only target of endorphins, but that the heart also responds to these proteins. In subsequent studies, Ventura discovered that the myocardial cells were able to synthesize and secrete endorphins. The heart was not only a target of endorphins, but for the first time it could be conceived as an endocrine organ capable of producing molecules that can modulate cellular homeostasis.

Ventura identified some of the genes responsible for the process of cardiac differentiation and found that the molecular signals underlying this differentiation were orchestrated by a complex system of endorphins that coordinate the orientation of stem cells towards the heart.[39] Thus, an adult myocardial cell retains a "memory" of the molecular mechanisms responsible for its own differentiation during the embryonic period of life.

These results, as well as opening the way for future cell therapy approaches of cardiac damage due to stroke or hereditary heart diseases, indicate that endorphins, which play a key role in many brain functions, also have a crucial impact in the process of heart differentiation and architecture and in the subsequent maintenance of cardiac function. The idea of a heart-brain axis originated from these findings. This axis would

---

39. Ventura, C. (2003), Zinellu, E., Maninchedda, E., Maioli, M., "Dynorphin B is an agonist of nuclear opioid receptors coupling nuclear protein kinase c activation to the transcription of cardiogenic genes in GTR1 embryonic stem cells," *Circ. Res.*, 92, 623–629.

be essential in determining and maintaining the balance of life. Modern developments in molecular biology are providing increasing evidence for the existence of a structure that links heart and brain from the earliest stages of embryonic development, through a "dialogue" between the molecular components that orient stem cells toward differentiation into neural precursors and heart.

Ventura points out that the link between the heart and the brain has been known in all ancient cultures, particularly in the East where it was believed that "the heart can affect the mind which can get down into the heart." This interpretation seems contrary to the Western scientific view that focuses on the structural and functional characteristics of the different organs. Ventura insists that the most recent discoveries of cellular and molecular biology suggest a new scenario where the development of the nervous and cardiovascular systems occur through the coordinated action of common attractors that drive the differentiation and migration of future cardiovascular and neuronal cells.

Recent studies show a strong parallelism in the development of both systems and indicate the existence of a two-way molecular interaction between stem cells that turn into myocardial and vascular progenitors and neurons.[40] Many molecules that play a crucial role in neurogenesis (e.g. retinoic acid, sonic hedgehog, bone morphogenetic proteins) and many transcription factors (molecules that can regulate the activity of genes in the DNA), are activated by the presence of these molecules and are essential for both neurogenesis and for cardiogenesis. In addition, both forms of differentiation represent early embryogenesis and embryonic developments that occur in very close areas known as the *cardiogenic field* and the *neurogenic field*, with continuous exchange of growth factors and molecular signals.

During the earliest stages of embryonic development the progenitors of neurogenesis and cardiogenesis establish an integrated network of molecular signals that persists during the later stages of development of the cranial-caudal axis of the embryo. This dialogue leaves deep memory traces that persevere into adult life since endorphins play a role in the development of the central nervous system. The same endorphins are expressed in the adult heart, where they control many molecular processes responsible for the contractile activity of myocardial cells and hypertrophy and accretion of the heart muscle. Other

---

40. Prigatano, G.P. (2003), "Challenging dogma in neuropsychology and related disciplines," *Archives of Clinical Neuropsychology*, 2003, 18: 811–825.

findings[41] also show that in totipotent stem cells endorphins control complex molecular signals that promote the cardiogenesis, i.e. the cardiac differentiation of stem cell populations, indicating that the adult myocardial cells retain a memory of the molecular system that had served to specify their architecture and function during the embryonic stage of life. This is the same system of endorphins that plays a decisive role in neuronal differentiation during embryogenesis and intervenes in the control of decisive functional adaptations of the adult central nervous system, such as memory, learning, pleasure, pain modulation, and attention.

This close link between the heart and the brain highlights the importance of including the heart as central to the study of consciousness. Shifting focus from the brain to the heart, and attention from the objective to the subjective, would constitute a major cultural revolution. The great Eastern traditions have developed sophisticated techniques to block the inner chatter of the mind and break the vicious cycle that keeps us tied to the perception of the exteriority of life. This condition of being-without-thinking enhances our awareness and leads to the realization that we draw our strength and vitality from our heart.

---

41. Perbellini, A., Ventura, C., and Maioli, M., (2004), "Use of Retinoic Esters of Hyaluronic Acid for the Differentiation of Totipotent Stem Cells," Retrieved from http://patentscope.wipo.int/search/en/WO2004063364.

Silence empowers this link, felt as love and experienced as feelings of warmth and wellbeing that nourish regenerative and healing processes. When we shift from brain activity, based on words, to that of the heart, based on feelings, thoughts start flowing silently. We feel our heart and at the same time we think. We are connected to the attractor and at the same time we can act in the physical reality. The thought of the heart requires that we accept the existence of a level of reality that is invisible to our material senses, a plane that transcends the physical reality, one in which we are guided. In the profound words of Ravi Ravindra:

> If we can sit with an increasing stillness of the body, and attune our mind to the sky or to the ocean or to the myriad stars at night, or any other indicators of vastness, the mind gradually stills and the heart is filled with quiet joy.[42]

---

42. Ravindra, R. (2009). *The Wisdom of Pantanjali's Yoga Sutras: A New Translation and Guide*. Sandpoint, ID: Morning Light Press.

# 13 VITAL NEEDS

According to the entropy/syntropy theory, life stems from the probabilistic quantum world. When it enters the macroscopic level, however, which follows forward-in-time causality, it becomes more deterministic and starts acting more in accordance with the law of entropy that eventually tends to destroy order or organization. The discovery of the law of entropy has turned life into a highly unlikely episode that does not stem from the laws of the universe. Syntropy, on the other hand, reintroduces life into the laws of the universe through the manifestation of the backward-in-time solution of the fundamental equations of the universe.

Entropy destroys life; syntropy constructs life. This consideration leads to the formulation of one of the fundamental laws of life: *In order to survive, life must always reduce entropy and increase syntropy*. From this derives the theory of vital needs,[43] which can be grouped in three main categories: material needs, the need for meaning, and needs for cohesion and love.

---

43. Di Corpo, U. (2007), "The Vital Needs Model," *Syntropy*, 1, pp. 147–158

## MATERIAL NEEDS: COMBATING THE DISSIPATIVE EFFECTS OF ENTROPY

In order to protect themselves from the dissipative effects of entropy, living systems must acquire energy from the outside. These conditions are generally referred to as *material needs*, or basic needs, and include combating the dissipative effects of entropy; for example, acquiring energy from the outside world through food, water, and air, and reducing the dissipation of energy with shelter and clothing. They also include the disposal of wastes caused by the law of entropy, i.e. hygiene and sanitation.

Complete satisfaction of these needs leads to a state characterized by the reduction of physical and emotional suffering. Partial satisfaction is experienced as relief of hunger, thirst, and disease. The complete lack of them, however, eventually leads to death. The satisfaction of material needs does not stop entropy from destroying the structures of living systems. For example, cells die and must be replaced. To repair the damages caused by entropy, living systems must draw on the regenerative properties of syntropy that allow it to create order, regenerate structures, and increase the level of organization. They must, therefore, acquire syntropy. In human beings this function is performed by the autonomic nervous system that supports such vital functions as heart activity or digestion.

Since syntropy acts as an absorber and concentrator of energy, it is felt as feelings of warmth in the area where the autonomic nervous system is located (heart/lungs/thorax), and associated with a sense of wellbeing. These feelings coincide with the experiences usually named *love*.

## THE NEED FOR MEANING: THE OPPOSITION OF ENTROPY AND SYNTROPY

In order to meet material needs, living systems have developed cortical structures that produce representations of the world that allow us to deal with the environment, but they give rise to a paradoxical opposition between entropy and syntropy. Entropy expands the universe towards the infinite (diverging forces), whereas syntropy concentrates the feeling of life, the Self, in extremely limited spaces. Consequently, when we compare ourselves with the infinity of the universe, we discover we are virtually nothing. On one side we feel we exist, on the other side we are aware of being irrelevant. These two opposing considerations generate the identity conflict described by Shakespeare as "to be, or not to be: that is the question." We must therefore solve the conflict between "to be or not to be" by finding meaning in life, although the strategies implemented to meet this need may differ. For example, we might try to increase our value through wealth, power, achievement, or the approval of others, or we might try to find meaning through ideologies and religions. The identity conflict is characterized by feelings of nothingness and meaninglessness, by lack of energy, existential crises, and depression. These feelings are generally perceived in the form of tension in the head and are generally associated with anxiety and anguish.

A famous experiment of Stanley Milgram[44] demonstrated how we seek meaning through the approval of others and how strong this need for positive judgment can be. The aim of this experiment was to determine the extent to which people were willing to obey orders to harm another person in order to obtain approval by the experimenter. Volunteers were instructed to administer electric shocks to a person in another room whenever they gave an incorrect response to a question. (They were unaware of the fact that the other person was really a collaborator of Milgram's and did not receive any actual electric shocks.) The volunteer was informed that the shock intensity had to be increased with each mistake. At 75 volts the collaborator began to complain, and at 150 he asked to stop the experiment, but the volunteer was told to continue, even when the collaborator began to scream and beg to be freed because he could no longer bear the pain. More than 80% of the participants continued the experiment even after they were begged to stop.

---

44. Milgram, S. (1974). *Obedience to Authority: An Experimental View.* New York: HarperCollins.

# 14 THE THEOREM OF LOVE

Syntropy determines our identity, our consciousness, or Self, which is small and cohesive, whereas entropy is the diverging outside Universe inflating towards infinity. Our ultimate goal is to unite ourselves with the Universe, a process named the *theorem of love*. This theorem posits that the interaction and union of entropy and syntropy is achieved through love, the aim, the attractor of life, which accomplishes the transition from duality to non-duality. It explains why anxiety (the lack of love) and depression (the lack of meaning) are so strongly correlated, although they have different etiologies.

In a keynote speech, for a 2007 forum on "Survival in an Orwellian World," Ayten Aydin noted that:

> The most important underlying factor of this anti-survival behavior of human beings is a combination of (among other things) greed, hatred and ideologies. All these vices, separately or combined, fuel ever-spreading acts of societal disintegration and the creation of two major camps in terms of controllers and the controlled.

> These vices are speedily gaining increased power fuelled by increasing hatred, which kills the ability to reason as well as inherent human wisdom, and thus strengthens and deepens further their belief systems.[45]

Often, when we desire to meet the expectations of others, we behave in ways that we believe others will judge positively, even when such behavior runs counter to our own nature, as in the Milgram experiment. When doing so, we use masks with which others interact rather than responding our true selves, which can result in increasing our feelings of loneliness and identity conflict. This is not to deny the fact that we need other people, but attributing our source of value and meaning to others generates a deep fear of being rejected. This social pressure and the fear of being marginalized can lead to the acceptance of conditions and values that the group imposes, rather than those that stem from our own key ethical values. Accepting the values of others can appear to provide meaning and can become vital to us, but it becomes easy to feel the need to defend these sources of identity and stay entrapped in their ideologies.

---

45. Aydin, A. (2007), "A culture of optimization and reconciliation: a concept of equitable, ethical and creative living," Keynote speech: IIAS Forum 2007 on "Survival in an Orwellian World."

Related to the need for positive judgment is a strategy based on the equivalence: *"I am since I have."* Having more money, popularity and power can give us the illusion that we are more. But when we substitute the need for meaning with the need for money, popularity, or power, these secondary needs create a distance between ourselves and others and trigger the fear of being deprived of what we possess. The theory of vital needs points out that these are nothing more than strategies to try to give a meaning to our life. There is no "biological" need for power, for popularity or money, but there is a real need for meaning.

Many people substitute their vital need for meaning with a religion. But the unconscious mind soon becomes aware of the fact that while this may provide power to religious institutions, organized religion is frequently unable to provide a personal meaning to life. In fact, it can even produce fear and hate towards those who belong to different religions. Throughout the history of humankind and in practically all cultures and nations the strength and power of organized religion has resulted in many wars and massacres conducted in the name of one fundamentalist religion or another.

According to the theory of vital needs, a sense of meaning and feelings of warmth and wellbeing are the needle of a compass that points to what is beneficial for our future, whereas feelings of chill and distress tell that we are on a wrong path or in dangerous territory. Learning to recognize and understand such feelings can therefore be of great help. There is empirical evidence that it is possible to intuit dangerous events in the future and avoid them. For example, in 1956 William Cox studied the number of tickets sold in the United State for commuter trains between 1950 and 1955 and found that in the 28 cases in which commuter trains had serious accidents a lower number of tickets was sold.[46] Even checking for possible intervening variables such as weather conditions, departing time, day of the week, etc., which could account for the accidents and the lower number of passengers, the reduction of ticket sales associated with the accidents continued to remain statistically significant. Cox's findings can be explained within the syntropy model in terms of subtle feelings of pain and distress being sent backward-in-time and felt in the present as premonitions or hunches that may lead to a decision not to travel. This backward-in-time flow of feelings can therefore change the future. Similar accounts are associated with airplane crashes. For example, Air India Express 812 flying between Dubai and Mangalore on 22 May 2010, crashed during landing, killing 158 passengers; only eight occupants survived the accident. After check-in,

---

46. Cox, W.E. (1956), "Precognition: An analysis," *Journal of the American Society for Psychical Research*, 1956(50): 99–109.

nine passengers felt ill and had refused to board the plane.[47] There have also been numerous reports of people who inexplicably changed their plans on the morning of 9/11.

We live in a time that disregards the body language of the autonomic nervous system. When we feel anxiety or anguish we might search for a substance (i.e. a cigarette, a glass of wine, a drug) or anything else that can free us from this uncomfortable experience. Anxiety, however, is an important indicator that something in our behavior needs to be adjusted. For example, when we feel thirsty we do not try to suppress this feeling since we know that dehydration would continue and could lead towards serious damage. Similarly, anxiety and anguish tell us that we have a shortage of syntropy and that we need to change our course.

Feelings propagate towards the past, but usually with no information associated with them. The anticipatory feelings of anguish and distress may take the form of feelings of anxiety without an object. They can also be caused by memories of past traumatic events, associated with the fear that these past traumas might happen again. We are thus constantly faced with the difficulty of distinguishing between anticipatory anxiety and anxiety caused by memories. The distinction

---

47. Retrieved from http://en.wikipedia.org/wiki/Air_ India_ Express_Flight_812.

between anguish and anxiety is probably that anguish indicates a lack of acquisition of syntropy, whereas anxiety anticipates future experiences of anguish. Anxiety, anguish, fear or panic, can all be such indicators. Although they may stem from different emotions, they all use similar signals.

Simply put, the vital need for syntropy is a need for cohesion and love. An insufficient intake of syntropy is experienced as feelings of emptiness, sometimes accompanied by such symptoms of the autonomic nervous system as nausea, dizziness, or feelings of suffocation, pain and suffering. Anguish is usually coupled with anxiety, which alert us in advance to future feelings of anguish.

For many people, the problem is not how to be happy and live fully every day, but how to let another day go by without too much suffering. Often we bind ourselves to others not for love, but because we fear loneliness, silence, and anxiety. The others thus become mere "objects" that we use as an escape from inner suffering. Individuals can be extremely clever and skilled in rejecting any awareness of the lack of syntropy. They may get involved in activities, avoid free time and moments of silence, or take refuge in conformism. Some may resort to stratagems like the use of substances that produce feelings of warmth in the solar plexus, such as alcohol, tobacco, and drugs, which can result in addiction. Others fill their lives with activities and commitments, and in their rare moments of relaxation or inner silence they immediately seek distractions in order to avoid their inner distress. But these strategies do not satisfy the very real need for love and cohesion, and as a result the acquisition of syntropy continues to be insufficient and the anguish persists.

Negative feelings, even though painful, are necessary to orient and guide our choices towards wellbeing. They are important signals that we must learn to listen to and understand in order to evolve towards a state of greater wellbeing and happiness. Eliminating negative feelings by artificial means without resolving the root cause can cause the body to enter a state of chronic lack of syntropy and reduce our ability to feel the future and choose advantageously. Perhaps most importantly, the lack of syntropy reduces our ability to feel another person's heart, thereby hindering those relationships that are the most essential source of syntropy.

# 15 THE MYSTERY OF LIFE

The ancient Greeks believed that life arose spontaneously from inorganic matter as a result of the action of the goddess Gaia. The question of how life can develop from non-living molecules was reformulated by the Latins as *generatio spontaneous*. In contemporary science, this hypothesis is known as *abiogenesis*.

It was not until mid-nineteenth century that the French chemist Louis Pasteur put the debate between biogenesis and abiogenesis to rest. By passing air through cotton filters, he demonstrated that the air is full of microorganisms and he realized that if these bacteria were present in the air then they would likely land on and contaminate any material exposed to it. The debate prompted the French Academy of Sciences to allocate a prize for anyone able to provide a convincing and accurate experimental answer to the question of how life can arise from non-living substance. Pasteur entered the contest with experiments that used heat to kill the microbes and his results were published in 1862, where he summarized his findings in the Latin phrase *Omnevivum ex vivo*, indicating that life can only be generated from living organic matter, and restricted the abiogenetic hypothesis to those special conditions that would have characterized the earliest stages of our planet Earth.[48]

In 1924, Alexander Oparin published a work in Russian entitled *The Origins of Life*[49] in which he described characteristics of colloids that demonstrate the ability to bind substances to their surfaces and suggests the beginning of metabolism. His book ends with the statement:

> Work is already in a very advanced stage, and soon the last barriers between organic and inorganic will fall under the attack of a patient work and powerful scientific theories.

The term *cosmochemistry*, or chemical cosmology, was coined by Harold Urey in 1952 to indicate the origin and development of the chemical elements on Earth and other planets during their evolution. (A closely related field is *astrochemistry*, a branch of astronomy concerned with measuring chemical elements in other parts of our own and other galaxies.) In his book *The Planets: Their Origin and Development*,[50] Urey deduced that the

---

48. Retrieved from http://en.wikipedia.org/wiki/Biogenesis

49. Oparin, A. (1924). *The Origin of Life*, Retrieved from http://www.uv.es/orilife/textos/The%20Origin%20of%20Life.pdf

50. Urey, H. (1952). *The Planets: Their Origin and Development.* Yale University Press.

composition of the primordial atmosphere should be made of methane ($CH_4$), ammonia ($NH_3$), nitrogen (N2), water ($H_2O$) and hydrogen ($H_2$). A student of Urey's, Stanley Miller, published an article three years later titled "A Production of Amino Acids Under Possible Primitive Earth Conditions"[51] in which he demonstrated that in a primordial atmosphere and in the presence of water, the action of electrical discharges (simulating the action of lightning) could generate amino acids, the fundamental building blocks of proteins. He proposed that the synthesis of amino acids could provide the building blocks for proteins, including some of those found in living systems. Miller termed this aqueous mixture *primordial soup*.

A question that then naturally arises is: *How did molecules that are essential for life form from amino acids?* Although amino acids are the building blocks of life, they are not considered to be living forms. Miller's experiments gave rise to a host of other experiments, still being conducted, which attempt to demonstrate the feasibility of constructing complex organic molecules from amino acids, but the results so far have been very problematic. For example, proteins involved in the metabolism of cells are composed of chains that include more than 90 amino acids. Simple combinatory calculations show that more than $10^{600}$

---

51. Miller, S.L. (1953), "A Production of Amino Acids under Possible Primitive Earth Conditions," *Science*, May 15.

(one followed by 600 zeroes!) permutations are required in order to arrive at the "spontaneous" formation of just one protein of 90 amino acids combining amino acids simply by chance. In an article published in the *American Scientist* in 1969, W. M. Elsasser concluded that the possibility of the spontaneous formation of just one protein is virtually nil, and noted that "the notion of mechanical causation in biology is devoid of logical underpinning" and that "the use of mechanism in life and ecology is metaphorical at best, and a very real danger exists that the use of this metaphor can too easily divert one's attention in the wrong direction."[52] Another problem is that primordial soups are made up mostly of water, but water leads to the decomposition of macromolecules and makes it impossible for amino acids to chain together in the initial stages of protein formation. The production of proteins in laboratories thus appears to be unsuitable for the formation of living organisms.

This leads to a third question about life: *What differentiates the organic from the inorganic?* Miller's experiments represented an important first step towards the synthesis of the molecules that are necessary for life, but have also led to an impasse. The synthetic production of proteins requires

---

52. Elsasser, W.M. (1969), "A causal phenomena in physics and biology: A case for reconstruction." *American Scientist*, 57: 502-16.

complex procedures of isolation and purification that do not occur spontaneously in nature and are based on hypotheses and experiments that derive from the study of living systems. These models involve theoretical assumptions about the relationship between inanimate matter and life that are defined by various fundamental characteristics of living organisms, such as the intake of substances and energy from the environment, metabolism, reproduction, growth, mobility, reaction to stimuli, and processing of information. Although the description of molecular structures can accommodate some physical characteristics of organisms and biochemical processes, it only identifies some of the requisite aspects of living systems. This limited understanding of the details and reciprocal interactions of molecules and macromolecules involved in the creation of living organisms (i.e. proteins or DNA), has not yet solved the mystery of life. We know about life only in relation to its material components, but still lack the knowledge of how DNA macromolecules, for example, can perform their functions only within the highly structured complexity of a cell. This indispensable whole is a prerequisite for life, and requires an approach that takes complexity into account. An unambiguous definition of life therefore is still missing.

Can the entropy/syntropy theory resolve this impasse?

# 16 THE LIMITS OF EVOLUTIONARY THEORY

## CLASSIFICATION AND TAXONOMY

Cataloging and classifying living organisms is one of the earliest objectives of biology and is referred to as *"taxonomy,"* from the Greek words *taxis* (ordering) and *nomos* (rule). In biology, a taxon (the plural is taxa) is a group of morphologically distinguishable organisms that are genetically recognizable from others as a unit with a precise location within the hierarchy of the taxonomic classification. Carl Linnaeus, the father of taxonomy, based the classifications primarily on the external features of living things, a procedure sometimes referred to as *Linnaean taxonomy*. Only later was taxonomy expanded to include anatomy, i.e. the skeleton and soft parts, and molecular and genetic information. Morphological taxonomy attempts to classify living beings according to their similarities, using neutral and objective descriptions.

Taxonomy is an empirical science that uses ranks including, among others: kingdom, phylum, class, order, family, genus, and species. In zoology, the nomenclature for the more important ranks is strictly regulated by the ICZN Code (International

Commission on Zoological Nomenclature), whereas taxonomy itself is never regulated, but is always determined by scientific research. How researchers arrive at their taxa varies depending on the available data, and resources and methods can range from simple quantitative or qualitative comparisons of striking features to elaborate computer analyses of large DNA sequences. For this reason, researchers can produce different classifications due to a series of subjective choices such as which features are chosen for consideration.

Genetic taxonomy was developed to overcome the limitations of subjective choices. The genetic approach classifies species according to their ability to produce fertile offspring under conditions of natural life, based on the idea that couples that produce fertile progeny belong to the same taxa. If organisms produce fertile offspring only when artificially crossed, in captivity or breeding, they are regarded as different species. For example, a mule is the product of an artificial cross between a horse and donkey, and is barren. The genetic approach therefore leads to catalog horses and donkeys as different species.

Biological taxonomy is therefore divided mainly into morphological taxonomy, which takes into account the external features (*morphospecies*), and genetic taxonomy, which takes into account fertility (*genospecies*). Depending on whether the emphasis is placed on the genetic (fertility) or morphological (features), the boundaries between species can vary. In the case of donkeys and horses there are two genospecies and one morphospecies, since they are indistinguishable on the basis of their external features, and therefore belong to the same morphospecies, but as they do not produce fertile offspring they do not belong to the same genospecies. To overcome this discrepancy, the base type classification was introduced, which takes into account both classifications. Even the base type classification, however, has not managed to produce generally accepted taxa. The geneticist W. Gottschalk says "Despite decades of research, the definition of species as a biological unit presents great difficulties. To date there is still no single definition that meets all the requirements."[53] The common definitions of species, genospecies, morphospecies, and base type, are imprecise because they do not permit a clear and always valid delineation among taxa. By applying different definitions of species, the boundaries inevitably change, raising the question of whether it is possible to define higher taxonomic units that encompass the concepts of both genetic and morphological species.

---

53. Gottschalk, W. (1994). *Allegmeine Genetick*, Stoccarda.

## MICRO AND MACRO-EVOLUTION

The terms microevolution and macroevolution were introduced in 1927 by Philiptschenko,[54] where *microevolution* indicates the selection of features within the same species; for example, quantitative changes of organs and structures of existing bodies. *Macroevolution* describes the evolution of new features; for example, the development of organs, structures, and forms of organization with qualitatively new genetic material. The function of microevolution is to optimize existing structures, while the function of macroevolution would be to develop structures with new functions.

An example of microevolution would be seeds carried by wind that typically fail to germinate in soils polluted by heavy metals. Occasionally, however, a small subset of the seeds may germinate, grow, and produce seeds that can colonize soils polluted by heavy metals. But these offspring are unable to re-cross with their parental plants and, based on the definition of genospecies, one might therefore say that a new species is born. Genetic analysis, however, shows that these new plants have not developed a new character, but rather a tolerance to the high content of heavy metals. The genetic information has therefore

---

54. Philiptschenko, J. (1927). *Variabilitat und Variation*, Berlin.

been limited, not altered, and it is therefore not considered an evolutionary progress due to new information.

Another example of microevolution is the cheetah, the fastest mammal on the planet. Despite its extraordinary abilities as a predator, the cheetah is endangered because of its very low genetic variability, which makes all members of the species very similar. This specialization leads to a susceptibility to illnesses, a high percentage of abnormal sperm, and the fact that after hunting these predators are so tired that they become unable to defend themselves or their prey from other competitors such as lions, leopards and hyenas. As a result, they have an insufficient capacity for adaptation, which increases their risks of extinction.

Examples of this type indicate that the process of microevolution should not be considered a development towards higher forms, but rather an impoverishment of the existing genetic information, and when this process of selection is repeated, it results in yet further depletion of the genetic information. As a result, while the new breeds may be more specialized and better suited to specific environments, as a result the species actually becomes weaker and less adaptable to environmental changes and more at risk of extinction.

According to Darwin's Origin of Species,[55] only random variations (mutations) that directly or indirectly benefit the possibilities of survival and contribute to evolutionary progress are selected, whereas deleterious mutations are mostly eliminated. Natural selection and genetic drift, i.e. the recombination of parental genes during sexual reproduction, are the key elements of the evolutionary process, but it is generally accepted that the mechanisms of natural selection and genetic drift operate only within the context of microevolution. Speciation, the formation of new species, is based on the loss of genetic information, and genetic drift does not produce anything new, but merely leads to the formation of a virtually unlimited number of new combinations of the same genetic material.

Unlike microevolution, macroevolution requires mechanisms that can increase and produce new information. Evolutionary factors such as natural selection, genetic drift, and isolation do not provide explanations for macroevolution. Consequently, the term has been, and still is understood in very different ways:

1. Some authors use it to indicate mechanisms other than Darwin's gradualism, which are

---

55. Darwin, C. (1859). *On the Origin of Species by Means of Natural Selection*, London; 2nd edition, Cambridge: Harvard University Press, 1964

insufficient to explain the development of new complex organs (such as the development of wings or legs, etc.).

2. Others use it in a descriptive way, without any comment on the mechanisms.

3. Sometimes it is used to indicate evolution beyond the species level, and the difference between microevolution and macroevolution becomes the border between species.

4. Occasionally a distinction is made by discipline—macroevolution is studied by paleontologists, microevolution by biologists.

5. And others reject the term macroevolution on the grounds that there is only one evolutionary mechanism.

The boundaries between microevolution and macroevolution are thus unspecific, and it is not possible to distinguish between these two terms.

In nature, genetic mutations appear spontaneously without apparent causes, and they can also be artificially induced or favored, for example by treatment with chemicals, radiation and temperature changes. Artificial mutations, however, limit evolution to the domain of microevolution. Empirical findings show that these mutations help explain the separation of a parental species into two or more species (speciation), but they do not explain the resulting increase in information. Offspring specialize in different directions, but cannot increase their information. One wonders then

a) if there are known mechanisms that explain macroevolution;

b) if there are clues that suggest that macroevolution is possible; and

c) if the equation *microevolution + time = macroevolution* is correct.

In natural selection a series of mutations should initiate the development of a new organism (macroevolution) that would survive only if every single change caused a selective advantage or, at least, not a disadvantage. This means that the evolution of a new organ or structure cannot go through intermediate stages that are disadvantageous and thus are unlikely to survive the process of natural selection. Since living systems must be able to survive in each stage of the evolutionary process, it becomes difficult to explain the development of complex organs. In general, the formation of new organs and structures and the biological value of selective advantage arises only after their completion and only when the various functions can interact. In computations or biological models, information on mechanisms, rates of mutation and recombination, suitable and appropriate selection criteria, and population size need to be introduced artificially, and cannot account for intermediate stages of evolution that have been observed in nature. There is no known natural process that can provide these resources.

Darwin's hypothesis requires the existence of numerous intermediate links that should testify to the evolutionary process between chimpanzees and humans, but such links have not yet been found and phylogenetic theory cannot completely ignore the fact that these links are missing. Evolutionary biologists try to explain their absence by saying that the evolutionary processes took place in marginal populations with a low probability of fossilization, yet paleontologists have provided evidence of a substantial consistency of species. For example, the major groups of plants apparently appeared quite suddenly and not in a gradual way, and species often appear in the wrong chronological order with the most complex and more highly evolved appearing first. The theory of macroevolution also maintains that affinities should be interpreted as convergences. But how can an evolutionary process without a tendency to converge towards similar results occur? Convergence is usually explained by saying that evolution has been strongly channeled by similar selective processes, but the fossil record shows that with regard to size, morphology, ecology, stages of development, and reproduction, old species cannot be distinguished from recent ones.

# 17 CONVERGING EVOLUTION

At the beginning of chapter 21, in his second book *The Descent of Man,* published 12 years after *The Origin of Species*, Darwin wrote:

> It seemed worthwhile to try how far the principle of evolution would throw light on some of the more complex problems in the natural history of man. False facts are highly injurious to the progress of science, for they often endure long; but false views, if supported by some evidence, do little harm, for everyone takes a salutary pleasure in proving their falseness: and when this is done, one path towards error is closed and the road to truth is often at the same time opened.[56]

The "road to truth" suggests a possibility, in Darwin's view, towards a hidden converging, retro-causality, and the main postulate of the entropy/syntropy theory is that life converges towards

---

56. Darwin, C. (1871). *Descent of Man*. London: John Murray. Retrieved from http://www.amazon.com/dp/B004TS0PQS.

attractors that guide the evolution of life. It displays striking similarities with the converging evolution theory of Teilhard de Chardin, although the starting point is different. In his lifetime Teilhard was subjected to strong censorship because his model challenged science to consider a new type of causality that retro-acts from the future.

According to the entropy/syntropy theory, life is subject to a dual causality, efficient causality and final causality, and this is true for Teilhard also. In his view life was guided by final aims that converge in what he termed "the Omega Point." Both the entropy/syntropy theory and the Omega Point identify final causality with the Source of life and the energy of Love.

Teilhard described reality as being organized in three concentric spheres. The innermost is the final aim of the evolution of the universe, in which everything ultimately will be transformed into organic and conscious matter; it is also the closest to the Omega point. The outer sphere is the most distant from the Omega point and is the realm of inanimate matter. The middle sphere is the realm of life that does not yet reflect on itself, the biosphere. He observed that:

> Evolution cannot be measured along the line that goes from the infinitely small to the infinitely big, but according to the axis that goes from the infinitely simple to the

infinitely complex. We can represent evolution as distributed on concentric spheres, each of which has a radius that diminishes as complexity grows.[57]

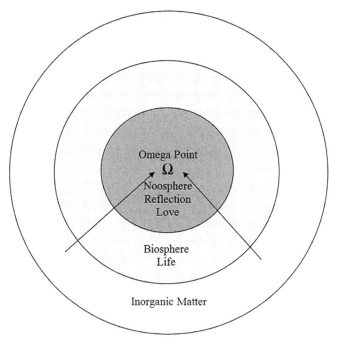

**Figure 8 – Teilhard's representation of reality organized as three concentric spheres.**

The theme of convergence became one of the fundamental concepts of Teilhard's vision. Working as a paleontologist, he showed that life evolves

---

57. Teilhard de Chardin, P. (2008). *Il fenomeno umano*. Brescia: Queriniana.

by converging towards attractors and that during this convergence process unity, complexity, and diversity increase. He related the Omega point to consciousness, which he considered the source of the Self, the feeling of life. In other words, the closer we evolve towards the final attractor the more conscious we become.

> The universe, taken as a whole, concentrates under the influence of the attraction which arises from the Omega point, which takes the form of love. People can evolve and become more human since they share at the core level the same attractor of love. According to this view we are all immersed in a converging flow of conscious energy, whose quality and quantity is growing at the same rhythm of our complexification.[58]

He viewed consciousness as a cosmological property of the universe that arises while converging towards unity and increasing complexity, in a process similar to that of syntropy:

> Consciousness increases in proportion to the complexity of life. Consciousness is absolutely inaccessible to our means of

---

58. Teilhard de Chardin, P. (2004). *Verso la convergenza. L'attivazione dell'energia nell'umanità*. Verona: Gabrielli Editori.

observation at the small level of viruses, but it clearly appears at the maximum level of complexity of the human brain.

Both Fantappiè and Teilhard explained macroevolution as a consequence of intelligent information provided by attractors, and ultimately by the Omega point, which would allow the sudden development of new organs without any intermediate evolutionary steps that would constitute a disadvantage. Attractors would inform our body and guide it to specific shapes and structures. Macroevolution would therefore be a converging retrocausal process.

A hypothesis that requires a different type of causality had also been postulated by Hans Driesch, a pioneer in experimental research in embryology. Driesch proposed the existence of final causes that act in a top-down way (from global to analytical, from the future to the past), and not in a bottom-up way as postulated in classical causality. Final causes would lead living matter to develop and evolve, and would coincide with the purpose of nature, the biological potential. Driesch named these final causes *entelechy*,[59] a Greek word whose derivation *(en-telos)* means something that contains within itself its own end or purpose,

---

59. Driesch, H. (1908). *The Science and Philosophy of the Organism*. London: Adam and Charles Black. Retrieved from http://www.gutenberg.org/ebooks/44388.

and that evolves towards this end. So if the path of normal development is interrupted, the system still can achieve the same end in another way. Driesch believed that the development and behavior of living systems are governed by a hierarchy of entelechies, all of which result in an ultimate entelechy. He demonstrated this phenomenon by dividing the cells of a sea urchin embryo after the first cell division, expecting each half cell to develop into the corresponding half of the animal for which it originally had been destined. Instead, he found that each part of the cell developed into a complete sea urchin. The same thing happened at the four-cell stage: entire larvae ensued from each of the four cells, albeit smaller than usual.

It is possible to remove large pieces from eggs, shuffle the blastomeres, and interfere with them in many ways without affecting the resulting embryo. It appears that any single monad in the original egg cell is capable of forming any part of the completed embryo. Conversely, when merging two young embryos, a single sea urchin results and not two sea urchins. These results show that sea urchins develop towards a single morphological end. When we act on an embryo, the surviving cell continues to respond to the final cause that leads to the formation of its destined structure. Although smaller, the structure achieved is similar to that which would have been obtained by the original embryo. From this it follows that the final form is not caused by a program or design that acts from the past, since any change we introduce in the past leads to the same future structure, even when a part of the system is removed or the normal development is disturbed.

Driesch also studied the process by which organisms are able to replace or repair damaged structures. For example, if a flatworm is cut into pieces each piece regenerates a complete worm. Many vertebrates also have extraordinary capabilities of regeneration. If the lens of a newt eye is surgically removed, a new lens is regenerated from the edge of the iris, whereas in the normal development of the embryo the lens is formed in a very different way, starting from the skin. Driesch used the concept of entelechy to account for the properties of integrity and directionality in the development and regeneration of bodies and living systems. Recent research into the properties of stem cells appears to confirm Driesch's ideas.

Independently, in 1926 the Russian scientist Alexander Gurwitsch[60] and the Austrian biologist Paul Alfred Weiss[61] proposed the existence of a factor they named *morphogenetic field*. The term comes from the Greek root morphe/morphic = form and

---

60. Gurwitsch, A.G. (1944). *The Theory of Biological Field*. Moscow: Soviet Science.

61. Weiss, P.A. (1939). *Principles of Development*. New York: Henry Holt and Company.

is used to emphasize the structural aspect. Apart from the claim that morphogenetic fields play an important role in the control of morphogenesis (the development of the shape of the body), neither author was able to show how causality works in these fields. The term "field" is often used to indicate something that is observed, but it is not yet understood in terms of classical causality. Events that require a new type of explanation require a different interpretation of "causality." The law of syntropy replaces the terms entelechy and field with the term attractor—a cause retroacting from the future that guides and generates a field.

In *A New Science of Life: The Hypothesis of Formative Causation*, biologist Rupert Sheldrake[62] refers to the theory of René Thom in "The Theory of Catastrophes," which identified the existence of attractors at the end of any evolutionary process.[63] Thom had introduced the idea that the shape of an organism could be due to causes that act from the future, and Sheldrake added the hypothesis of "formative causation," according to which morphogenesis is guided by attractors, i.e. retrocausal processes.

---

62. Sheldrake, R. (1981). *A New Science of Life: The Hypothesis of Formative Causation.* London: Blond & Briggs.

63. Thom, R. (1972). *Structural Stability and Morphogenesis.* W. A. Benjam.

Experimental results that can be explained in terms of attractors were provided by Sheldrake's observation that members of the same group, such as animals of the same species, are able to share knowledge without using any form of physical information transmission. For example, when a mouse learns a task, this same task is learned more easily by other mice of the same breed. The greater the number of mice that learn to perform a task, the easier it is for individual mice of that breed to learn the same task. For example, if thousands of mice are trained to perform a new task in a laboratory in London, similar mice learn to perform the same task more quickly in laboratories all over the world.[64] This effect occurs in the absence of any known physical connection or communication between the laboratories. The same effect is observed in the growth of crystals. In general, the ease of crystallization increases with the number of times that the operation is performed, even when there is no way in which these crystal nuclei may have been moved from one place to another infecting the different solutions.[65]

Sheldrake explains these results in terms of morphogenetic fields, which are a combination of the

---

64. Sheldrake, R. (2012). *The Science Delusion*. London: Cornet.

65. Sheldrake, R. and Fox, M. (2014). *The Physics of Angels: Exploring the Realm Where Science and Spirit Meet*, Monkfish.

concepts of fields and energy. Energy can be considered the cause of change; the field can be considered the way in which change is guided. Fields have physical effects, but are not themselves a type of energy, yet they guide energy in a geometric or spatial organization. The entropy/syntropy theory translates "fields" as "attractors" and concurs with Sheldrake's statement that morphogenetic fields (i.e. attractors) would be at the basis of formative causation, morphogenesis, evolution, and the maintenance of the shape of living systems at all levels of complexity, not only on the surface, but also in internal processes.

# 18 ATTRACTORS

*Attractors* provide the purpose, or "blueprint," of a system, and determine its ultimate shape and properties, similar to those of Driesch's entelechy. In a sense, the design might be compared to a field that corresponds to the system. It is not physically present, but it provides stability and allows the system to be expressed physically in accordance with the design. It is this cohesive force of syntropy that opposes the divergent force of entropy. This is true of cells, organs, trees, and living systems in general. For each species, for each type of cell and organ, there is at least one attractor that coincides with what could be called a morphogenetic field corresponding to the attractor that drives the living system towards a specific form and evolution.

Conrad Waddington coined the term *epigenetics* in 1942 to describe the branch of biology that studies the causal interactions between genes and phenotypes, i.e. the physical manifestation of the body.[66] According to epigenetics, phenotypes are the result of inherited genetic mutations that last

---

66. Waddington, C. H. (1942). *Science and Ethics*. London: George Allen & Unwin.

for the entire life of a living system and can be transmitted to subsequent generations through cell division. This hypothesis, that the features of life can be improved by means of random mutations, contradicts the law of entropy, however, according to which the spontaneous formation of the smallest molecule of protein requires at least $10^{600}$ mutations. It also implies that some mysterious mechanism has produced genetic programs and genetic instructions that guide the properties of life.

Attractors would provide such programs and instructions, and establish the common denominator of a collectivity of individuals. For example, the attractor "humanity" is the common denominator of all human beings; the attractor "mice" is the common denominator of all mice. Besides providing programs and instructions, attractors also act as relays of information. They receive the experiences of individuals, select what is advantageous for the species, and transmit it to all the other members of the species. This mechanism explains how when mice in a laboratory learn to solve a task, all the mice of the same species could solve the same task more easily. It also challenges the assumption that genes store information; rather, genes would act as antennae that connect the cells of an organism to the information in the attractor. When genes are broken the communication malfunctions, the system does not develop correctly, and disease emerges.

The *supercausal paradigm* reverses the traditional way of thinking since it proposes that intelligent causality provides programs and guidance from the future. Whereas causality produces effects that diverge from the past, retrocausality produces effects that converge towards attractors in the future.[67]

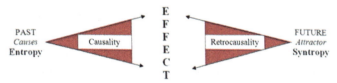

**Figure 9 – Supercausality**

This paradigm suggests that attractors continuously broadcast information non-locally, and that events interact through a process of information exchange. It posits that only information that enhances the possibility of a positive future for life is shared, enabling life in the Universe to converge towards a sort of intelligent causality. This bears some resemblance to the *anthropic principle* proposed by Barrow and Tipler,[68] which states that there is a mechanism that has attracted the Universe towards physical constants that happen to

---

67. Di Corpo, U. and Vannini, A. (2011). *Supercausality and complexity. Changing the rules in the study of causality.* Kindle Editions.

68. Barrow, J.D. and Tipler, F.J. (1988). *The Anthropic Cosmological Principle.* Oxford University Press.

fall within that narrow range that is compatible with life. Or, in other words, the Universe seems to be attracted towards those conditions that favor the eventual emergence of life.

While studying meteorological phenomena, in 1963 Edward Lorenz noted that small perturbations that react to slight variations in chaotic systems could amplify at each point in their evolution, making accurate weather forecasting virtually impossible. These events became known as *chaotic attractors*. In Lorenz's words: "The flap of a butterfly's wings in Brazil can set off a tornado in Texas."[69] This idea of a "butterfly effect" has since burgeoned in popular culture and has become a central tenet of chaos theory. It provides a striking analogy for how small actions can have tremendously powerful effects, often independent of the intent of the initial action.

When attractors interact with entropic or chaotic physical systems fractal geometry arises. The term *fractal* was coined by Benoît Mandelbrot[70] in 1975, and derives from the Latin word *fractus* (broken), similarly to the word fraction, since fractal images are fractional mathematical objects. They are

---

69. Lorenz, E.N. (1969),"Atmospheric predictability as revealed by naturally occurring analogues," *Journal of the Atmospheric Sciences* 26 (4): 636–646.

70. Mandelbrot, B.B. (1987). *Gli oggetti frattali*. Torino: Einaudi.

mathematical sets that exhibit a repeating pattern and are often found in complex dynamical systems and described using simple recursive equations. For example, the square root of a number greater than zero (but smaller than one) will tend toward one, but will never reach it. Number one is therefore the attractor of the square root. Similarly, if we continue to square a number greater than one, the result will tend to infinity. If the replication is exactly the same at every scale it is called a self-similar pattern. Fractal figures are obtained by inserting an attractor (which tends to a limit) into an entropic system.

Fractals are closely related to the work of Leonardo of Pisa, who wrote a book called *Liber Abaci*[71] (*The Book of Calculation*) in 1202 under the pen name "Fibonacci." This work proved a significant contribution to the history of mathematics because it introduced the use of Arabic numerals into Europe, which eventually replaced Roman numerals. He described a sequence of numbers that would come to be called Fibonacci Numbers, although this number sequence already had been used in Sanskrit poetry as early as 450 BC. He called this sequence *Modus Indorum* (method of the Indians), and applied it to solving a problem involving the growth of a population of rabbits based on idealized assumptions. The solution turned out to be

---

71. Pisano, Leonardo (2006), "Contributions to Number Theory." *Encyclopedia Britannica Online*.

a sequence of numbers that was the sum of each the two previous numbers. The ratio between the numbers in a Fibonacci sequence (1.618034) is sometimes called the Golden Ratio, or Golden Section, and can be found throughout nature.

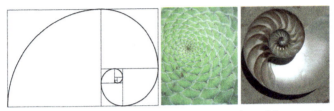

**Figure 10 – Fibonacci sequence and golden ratio**
Dicklyon/Wikimedia Commons; Max Ronnersjö/Wikimedia Commons; jChris 73/Wikimedia Commons

Fractal geometry reproduces some of the most important structures of living systems, and many researchers believe that life follows the principles of fractal geometry. The spiral shape of the Golden Ratio can be seen throughout nature—in the leaf arrangement in plants, the pattern of the florets of a flower, a grains of wheat, the growth of corals, a hive of bees, and in the form of the brain and neurons, as well as the lungs. All of these form trees with multiple ramifications and with configurations that are similar at both low and high magnification. The Fibonacci numbers may be nature's numbering system and appear to be applicable to the growth of every living thing.

Blood arteries and coronary veins also show fractal patterns as they divide into smaller vessels, which divide into yet smaller ones. It would

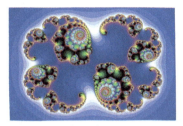 

**Figure 11 – Examples of fractal images**
Solkoll/Wikimedia Commons; Josep M. Batlle/Wikimedia Commons

appear that these fractal structures play an important role in the contraction and conduction of electrical stimuli. The spectral analysis of the heart frequency, for instance, shows that the normal frequency resembles a chaotic structure. All of these observations are consistent with the hypothesis that the organization and evolution of living systems is guided by attractors in a fashion similar to what happens in fractal geometry.

According to the entropy/syntropy theory, living species originate from the retro-action of attractors, possibly expressed through the unique properties of water, a vital property of all living systems. Life would therefore start in water, with primitive and essential structures and forms driven by the attractors that provide them with their shape and information, and survival would therefore be linked to the ability individuals to express the shape and the qualities already present in the attractor. According this view, every living species would have attractor. Rather than reflecting a tr from less evolved to higher species, th of evolution would develop in parallel, towards its own ends. Just as Michelangelo stated that the skill of an artist is to bring out from stone the figure that is already in it but does not belong to it, the entropy/syntropy theory proposes that the successful survival of a living system entails bringing forth the attractor that is already inherent in its body, but it does not belong to the body. Genes would serve the function of receiving information from attractors in the future rather than encoding it from the past.

Long before Darwin published *The Origin of Species*, scholars were divided into two main camps. One group included scientists and philosophers of the Age of Enlightenment, an 18th century movement whose goal was to advance knowledge and promote science and intellectual interchange, and who envisioned a dynamic and constantly changing nature. The other group, who believed in a substantially unchanging nature, espoused the theory of fixity proposed by Linnaeus that was rooted in the biblical Genesis and Aristotelian philosophy. For them, the various species and entities had been created once and for all and were unable to change. This debate continues to this day in the conflict between *evolutionists* who claim that life and its various forms emerged gradually as a result of mutation and natural selection over millions of years, and *creationists* who endorse the theory of Intelligent Design and believe that life in its various forms originated instantaneously some thousands of years ago through the mathematical sets that exhibit a repeating pattern and are often found in complex dynamical systems and described using simple recursive equations. For example, the square root of a number greater than zero (but smaller than one) will tend toward one, but will never reach it. Number one is therefore the attractor of the square root. Similarly, if we continue to square a number greater than one, the result will tend to infinity. If the replication is exactly the same at every scale it is called a self-similar pattern. Fractal figures are obtained by inserting an attractor (which tends to a limit) into an entropic system.

Fractals are closely related to the work of Leonardo of Pisa, who wrote a book called *Liber Abaci*[71] (*The Book of Calculation*) in 1202 under the pen name "Fibonacci." This work proved a significant contribution to the history of mathematics because it introduced the use of Arabic numerals into Europe, which eventually replaced Roman numerals. He described a sequence of numbers that would come to be called Fibonacci Numbers, although this number sequence already had been used in Sanskrit poetry as early as 450 BC. He called this sequence *Modus Indorum* (method of the Indians), and applied it to solving a problem involving the growth of a population of rabbits based on idealized assumptions. The solution turned out to be

---

71. Pisano, Leonardo (2006), "Contributions to Number Theory." *Encyclopedia Britannica Online*.

a sequence of numbers that was the sum of each the two previous numbers. The ratio between the numbers in a Fibonacci sequence (1.618034) is sometimes called the Golden Ratio, or Golden Section, and can be found throughout nature.

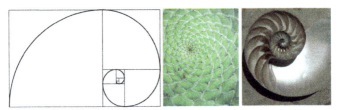

**Figure 10 – Fibonacci sequence and golden ratio**
Dicklyon/Wikimedia Commons; Max Ronnersjö/Wikimedia Commons; jChris 73/Wikimedia Commons

Fractal geometry reproduces some of the most important structures of living systems, and many researchers believe that life follows the principles of fractal geometry. The spiral shape of the Golden Ratio can be seen throughout nature—in the leaf arrangement in plants, the pattern of the florets of a flower, a grains of wheat, the growth of corals, a hive of bees, and in the form of the brain and neurons, as well as the lungs. All of these form trees with multiple ramifications and with configurations that are similar at both low and high magnification. The Fibonacci numbers may be nature's numbering system and appear to be applicable to the growth of every living thing.

Blood arteries and coronary veins also show fractal patterns as they divide into smaller vessels, which divide into yet smaller ones. It would fall within that narrow range that is compatible with life. Or, in other words, the Universe seems to be attracted towards those conditions that favor the eventual emergence of life.

While studying meteorological phenomena, in 1963 Edward Lorenz noted that small perturbations that react to slight variations in chaotic systems could amplify at each point in their evolution, making accurate weather forecasting virtually impossible. These events became known as *chaotic attractors*. In Lorenz's words: "The flap of a butterfly's wings in Brazil can set off a tornado in Texas."[69] This idea of a "butterfly effect" has since burgeoned in popular culture and has become a central tenet of chaos theory. It provides a striking analogy for how small actions can have tremendously powerful effects, often independent of the intent of the initial action.

When attractors interact with entropic or chaotic physical systems fractal geometry arises. The term *fractal* was coined by Benoît Mandelbrot[70] in 1975, and derives from the Latin word *fractus* (broken), similarly to the word fraction, since fractal images are fractional mathematical objects. They are

---

69. Lorenz, E.N. (1969),"Atmospheric predictability as revealed by naturally occurring analogues," *Journal of the Atmospheric Sciences* 26 (4): 636–646.

70. Mandelbrot, B.B. (1987). *Gli oggetti frattali*. Torino: Einaudi.

The *supercausal paradigm* reverses the traditional way of thinking since it proposes that intelligent causality provides programs and guidance from the future. Whereas causality produces effects that diverge from the past, retrocausality produces effects that converge towards attractors in the future.[67]

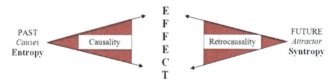

**Figure 9 – Supercausality**

This paradigm suggests that attractors continuously broadcast information non-locally, and that events interact through a process of information exchange. It posits that only information that enhances the possibility of a positive future for life is shared, enabling life in the Universe to converge towards a sort of intelligent causality. This bears some resemblance to the *anthropic principle* proposed by Barrow and Tipler,[68] which states that there is a mechanism that has attracted the Universe towards physical constants that happen to

---

67. Di Corpo, U. and Vannini, A. (2011). *Supercausality and complexity. Changing the rules in the study of causality.* Kindle Editions.

68. Barrow, J.D. and Tipler, F.J. (1988). *The Anthropic Cosmological Principle.* Oxford University Press.

develop in parallel, towards its own ends. Just as Michelangelo stated that the skill of an artist is to bring out from stone the figure that is already in it but does not belong to it, the entropy/syntropy theory proposes that the successful survival of a living system entails bringing forth the attractor that is already inherent in its body, but it does not belong to the body. Genes would serve the function of receiving information from attractors in the future rather than encoding it from the past.

Long before Darwin published *The Origin of Species*, scholars were divided into two main camps. One group included scientists and philosophers of the Age of Enlightenment, an 18th century movement whose goal was to advance knowledge and promote science and intellectual interchange, and who envisioned a dynamic and constantly changing nature. The other group, who believed in a substantially unchanging nature, espoused the theory of fixity proposed by Linnaeus that was rooted in the biblical Genesis and Aristotelian philosophy. For them, the various species and entities had been created once and for all and were unable to change. This debate continues to this day in the conflict between *evolutionists* who claim that life and its various forms emerged gradually as a result of random mutation and natural selection over millions of years, and *creationists* who endorse a theory of Intelligent Design and believe that life in its main forms originated instantaneously some thousands of years ago through the

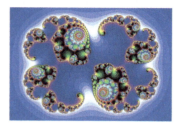 

**Figure 11 – Examples of fractal images**
Solkoll/Wikimedia Commons; Josep M. Batlle/Wikimedia Commons

appear that these fractal structures play an important role in the contraction and conduction of electrical stimuli. The spectral analysis of the heart frequency, for instance, shows that the normal frequency resembles a chaotic structure. All of these observations are consistent with the hypothesis that the organization and evolution of living systems is guided by attractors in a fashion similar to what happens in fractal geometry.

According to the entropy/syntropy theory, living species originate from the retro-action of attractors, possibly expressed through the unique properties of water, a vital property of all living systems. Life would therefore start in water, with primitive and essential structures and forms driven by the attractors that provide them with their shape and information, and survival would be therefore be linked to the ability of individuals to express the shape and the design already present in the attractor. According to this view, every living species would have its own attractor. Rather than reflecting a transition from less evolved to higher species, the process of evolution would act of God. Their argument is that the inability of Darwin's theory to explain macroevolution implies the agency of intelligent causality. But Intelligent Design does not explain macroevolution either; it only states that a different type of causality is required.

Can the entropy/syntropy theory resolve this debate?

# 19 THE BALANCING ROLE OF ENTROPY AND SYNTROPY

Entropy and syntropy are complementary properties of the same unity. In *Syntropy: Definition and Use,* Mario Ludovico writes:

> I deem it impossible to grasp the concept of syntropy without having assimilated the concept of entropy, since not only are the two concepts in a strict mutual connection but entropy and syntropy are also complementary concepts. In other words, where it is possible to measure a level of entropy there is a complementary level of syntropy.[72]

The concept of two complementary forces, one diverging and one converging, one visible and one invisible, one destructive and one constructive, can be found in many philosophies and religious traditions. In Taoist philosophy, for example, all aspects of the universe are regarded as the interplay of two fundamental principles: *yang*, which

---

72. Ludovico, M. (2008), "Syntropy: Definition and Use," *Syntropy*, 1: 139–201.

is convergent, and *yin*, which is divergent. These two influences constitute a unity and when one increases the other decreases, but their overall balance remains unchanged, and their interaction generates an energy called *chi*, a concept very similar to syntropy. This principle is beautifully represented in the Taijitu symbol, which shows the union and interaction of these two principles whose combined action is believed to move all aspects of the universe.

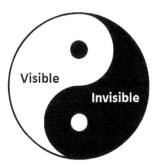

**Figure 12 – Taijitu symbol**

In Hinduism the same law of complementarity is symbolized by the cosmic dance of Shiva and Shakti, where Shakti is the personification of the feminine principle and is the energy of the visible physical world, and Shiva is the masculine principle, the ordering principle or consciousness that transcends the visible world. As in the Chinese Yin and Yang, each contains an aspect of the other. Shiva would thus represent the organizing properties of syntropy and come from the future, whereas Shakti, or time, would represent the disordering properties of entropy and flow from the past. Together they represent the dynamic organizing forces and the primordial cosmic energy that are expressed throughout the entire universe, and one cannot exist without the

**Figure 13 – The Cosmic Complementarity of Shiva and Shakti**

other. Sometimes they are even represented by a single figure called *Ardbanarisvara*, whose right side is male and whose left side is female.

It is not unusual for the action of syntropy to produce what appear as anomalous synchronicities. According to Carl Jung, these are experiences of two or more events that apparently are causally unrelated and unlikely to occur together by chance, yet are experienced subjectively as meaningful. In *Synchronicity: An Acausal Connecting Principle*,[73] published jointly with a related study by physicist Wolfgang Pauli, Jung described synchronicities as "temporally coincident occurrences of acausal events," or as causality that acts from the future. The concept does not question or compete with the notion of causality. Rather, it maintains that just as events may be grouped by causes, they may also be grouped by a meaningful principle of finalities. According

---

73. Jung, C.G. (1951). *Synchronicity: An Acausal Connecting Principle*, Princeton, NJ, Princeton University Press.

to Jung, synchronicity and causality are complementary and both derive from the same indestructible energy.

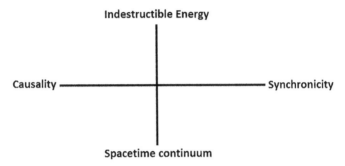

Figure 14 – Jung and Pauli representation of causality and synchronicity

This same complementarity can be observed in the process of metabolism, where *entropy* corresponds to *catabolic* processes that transform higher level structures into lower level ones through the release of chemical and thermal energy, and *syntropy* corresponds to *anabolic* processes that transform simple nutritive elements into complex bio-molecules through the absorption of energy. Syntropy concentrates energy by increasing order and organization, but since the concentration of energy cannot increase indefinitely, at some point the system releases energy and matter, and activates the processes of entropy and the exchange of energy and matter with the environment. Life naturally tends toward increased syntropy, but at the macroscopic level it is governed by the law of increasing entropy. Exchange between living systems and the environment results in a continuous process of construction and destruction that allows life to evolve, just as in the dance of Shiva and Shakti. This complementary exchange is a fundamental property of living systems at all levels of organization.

A good example of the complementarity between entropy and syntropy is the *torus*, an energy pattern where energy flows in one end, circulates around the center, and exits out the other side. It is usually invisible, but it can be seen by scattering iron filings loosely around a magnet. This pattern is evident in hurricanes, planets, suns, galaxies, and also within cells, flowers, trees and animals, and is the result of the interaction between diverging and converging forces.

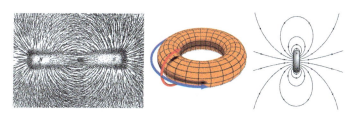

**Figure 15 – The torus pattern of energy**
Newton Henry Black/Wikimedia Commons; Dave Burke/Wikimedia Commons; Geek3/Wikimedia Commons

A similar process takes place in ecosystems, based on cycles of ascendancy and overhead. Ascendancy describes the tendency towards organized phenomena, overhead the flow of disorganized energy. In *A Third Window*, Ulanowicz[74] points out that "Real systems are the result of an ongoing transaction between the opposing tendencies of both ascendancy and overhead."

---

74. Ulanowicz, R.E. (2009). *A Third Window*. Templeton Foundation Press.

# 20 SYNTROPY ACTIVATION

Syntropy activation stems from the combination of the principle of complementarity and the vital needs theory and enables people and organizations to embrace and exploit change optimally. An open approach to change can lead to robust health, whereas a closed attitude can generate disease. Change is unavoidable over time, yet many people tend to be afraid of it and try to avoid it.

We can represent the complementarity between entropy and syntropy as a see-saw, where entropy and syntropy play at the opposite sides and when one decreases, the other rises. This see-saw representation can be divided into blocks according to the three vital needs, as in Figure 16, where

1. the left block is related to material needs and it is governed by the conscious mind and the law of entropy. It is the visible side of reality;

2. the central block is related to our need for meaning and it is governed by the unconscious mind which mediates the visible and invisible sides of reality; and

3. the right block is related to our immaterial need for syntropy and it is governed by the superconscious mind, intuitions and synchronicities.

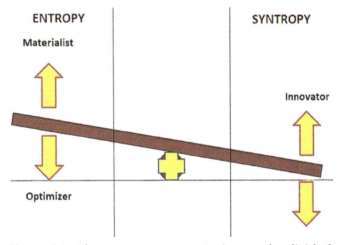

Figure 16 – The see-saw representation can be divided into 3 blocks

On the left side of the image, the reduction of entropy is achieved through a continuous tension towards optimization; on the right side, the increase in syntropy is obtained due to the process of intuition, a property of the superconscious mind. The interchange between the optimizer and the innovator together can lead towards a new vision of reality as the rational approach of the optimizer and the intuitive approach of the innovator play constantly together, continuously changing our perspective.

# 21 THE DUAL SOLUTION OF THE FUNDAMENTAL EQUATIONS OF PHYSICS

According to the Copenhagen interpretation of quantum mechanics, the act of observation forces the wave function to collapse into a particle. In other words, electrons and other atomic-level phenomena seem to be dependent upon the activity of consciousness. Reality is *created*, at least in part, by the observer.

Another curious property of atomic physics is that of *spin*, an angular momentum that can never be equal to zero. Therefore, when combining quantum mechanics and special relativity the full energy/momentum/mass equation needs to be considered. In 1925 physicists Oskar Klein and Walter Gordon formulated a probability equation that could be used in quantum mechanics and is relativistically invariant. The *Klein-Gordon equation* depends on a square root and yields two solutions. The positive solution describes waves that propagate from the past to the future (*retarded waves*), whereas the negative solution describes waves that propagate backward-in-time from the future to the past (*advanced waves*). Klein and Gordon explained the dual wave/particle nature of matter as the continuous interaction between retarded waves (the forward-in-time solution where causality is determined) and advanced waves (backward-in-time solution where retrocausality is probabilistic).

In 1928 English physicist Paul Dirac tried to eliminate the advanced wave solution by applying the energy/momentum/mass equation to the study of relativistic electrons. He was faced again with a dual solution: electrons ($e^-$) and neg-electrons ($e^+$, the anti-particle of the electron). The equation Dirac proposed predicted a universe made of matter that propagates forward-in-time, and antimatter which propagates backward-in-time:

> One gets over the difficulty on the classical theory by arbitrarily excluding those solutions that have a negative Energy. One cannot do this in the quantum theory.[75]

Dirac named the anti-particle of the electron a *neg-electron*, and in 1932 it was experimentally observed by Carl Anderson, who renamed it a *positron*.[76,77] Positrons are produced naturally in

---

75. Dirac, P.A.M. (1928), "The Quantum Theory of the Electron," *Proc. Royal Society*, London, 117:610-624; 118:351-361.

76. Anderson, C.D. (1932), "The apparent existence of easily deflectable positives," *Science*, 76:238.

77. Feynman, R.P. (1949), "The Theory of Positrons," *Physical Review* 76: 749.

certain types of radioactive decay. In 1934 the Swiss mathematician Ernst Stueckelberg, and later Richard Feynman, provided a formalism where each line of a diagram represents a particle propagating either backward or forward in time. This formalism is now a widespread method of computing quantum fields and is known as the Feynman-Stueckelberg interpretation of antiparticles.

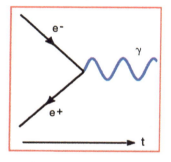

Figure 17 – In the diagram, arrows to the right represent electrons, arrows to the left represent positrons, and wavy lines photons.

Most physicists, however, still tend to reject the negative solution of the fundamental equations, and when faced with a choice implying a paradigm change they almost invariably opt for the alternative that is consistent with the prevailing viewpoint. The rejection of the negative energy solution, however, has made the two theories upon which all modern physics rests, relativity and quantum mechanics, seem incompatible, since when they are combined an unacceptable universe of backward-in-time energy arises.

Dirac's equation, Einstein's energy/momentum/mass equation, and the Klein-Gordon equation all call for symmetry between positive and negative energy: forces that blast matter apart and forces that bind matter together. Dirac's equation describes a field that contains unlimited symmetrical amounts of negative and positive energy. When approaching the zero-point, everything is bound closer together and negative energy becomes predominant. At the zero-point, however, instead of no energy there is suddenly a flood of it—real energy, with measurable effects. This implies that we are surrounded by an immense, all pervasive, yet virtually undetectable sea of zero-point energy with no mass and inertia or gravitational interaction, which allows for non-local effects that can propagate instantaneously.

# 22 THE PARADOX OF NON-LOCALITY

In 1935 Albert Einstein, Boris Podolsky, and Nathan Rosen published an article titled "Can Quantum-Mechanical Description of Physical Reality be Considered Complete?"[78] which has since become known as the *EPR Paradox*. It was originally proposed as a thought experiment, intended to demonstrate an inherent paradox in the early formulations of quantum theory called *quantum entanglement*, which describes a situation where multiple electrons are linked together in such a way that the measurement of one particle's quantum state determines the quantum states of the other particles at that exact same moment. It is paradoxical because the phenomenon seems to involve instantaneous communication between the two particles at speeds greater than the speed of light, thereby conflicting with relativity theory.

At the time it was proposed there was no way to actually carry out the experiment, but in 1952 David Bohm suggested replacing electrons with

---

78. Einstein, A., Podolsky, B., Rosen, N. (1935), "Can Quantum-Mechanical Description of Physical Reality be Considered Complete?" *Physical Review* 47 (10): 777–780.

photons, and in 1964 John Bell showed that the change introduced by Bohm opened the way to the possibility of an actual experiment. At that time even Bell did not believe that the experiment could be performed, but in 1982 Alain Aspect published the results of research that showed that Einstein was wrong and that non-locality was real.[79] As a consequence of Aspect's results, quantum mechanics and special relativity are now generally considered incompatible.

In 1978 John Wheeler proposed a variation of Aspect's double-slit experiment in which the photon detectors could be activated after the passage of a photon through one of two slits. With advanced technology, this delayed-choice experiment became possible and results demonstrated that this effect operates backward-in-time. In other words, our choice of how to measure the photon demonstrates that retrocausal effects operate at the quantum level.

Inspired by the absorber-emitter model developed by Wheeler and Feynman,[80] in 1986 John Cramer published *The Transactional Interpretation of*

---

79. Aspect, A. (1982), "Experimental Realization of Einstein-Podolsky-Rosen-Bohm Gedanken experiment," *Physical Review Letters*, vol. 49, 91, 1982.

80. Wheeler, J. and Feynman, R. (1945), "Interaction with the Absorber as Mechanism of Radiation," *Review of Modern Physics* (17).

*Quantum Mechanics*,[81] which allows a simple explanation of how the dual nature of matter (particles and waves) can accommodate non-locality and other mysteries of quantum mechanics and permit a unification of quantum mechanics with special relativity. Cramer pointed out that the probabilistic equation developed by Max Born in 1926 contains an explicit reference to the nature of time and to the two possible solutions that describe advanced and delayed waves.[82]

Even though classical physicists are still uncomfortable with retrocausality and the negative solution of the equations, several respected scientists currently are working on this possibility. In 2006 the American Institute of Physics organized a conference in San Diego California titled "Frontiers of Time: Retrocausation – Experiment and Theory," the proceedings of which contain more than 20 contributions on retrocausality.[83] And in November 2010, President Barack Obama awarded the National Medal of Science to physicist Yakir Aharonov for experimental studies that

---

81. Cramer, J.G. (1986), "The Transactional Interpretation of Quantum Mechanics," *Reviews of Modern Physics*, Vol. 58: 647–688.

82. De Beauregard, O.C. (1977), "Time Symmetry and the Einstein Paradox, I," *Nuovo Cimento*, 42B.

83. "Frontiers of Time: Retrocausation—Experiment and Theory," AIP, American Institute of Physics, Proceedings at http://scitation.aip.org/content/aip/proceeding/aipcp/863/.

show that the present is a result of causes flowing from the future as well as from the past. This research suggests a radical reinterpretation of time and causality.[84]

---

84. Aharonov, Y. (2005). *Quantum Paradoxes*. Berlin: Wiley-VCH.

# 23 DIVERGING AND CONVERGING CYCLES

The entropy/syntropy theory posits that any system, organic or inorganic, cycles between peaks of entropy and syntropy, acquiring in time specific resonances that can be observed at any level, from the quantum to the macroscopic, and even at the cosmological level as in the Big Bang/Big Crunch cycle.

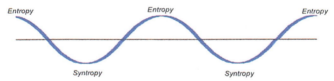

**Figure 18 – Entropy and Syntropy cycles**

The term *"Big Bang"* was coined by Fred Hoyle during a BBC radio broadcast in March 1949 to describe an immense explosion that was the origin of our universe. The first formulation of the Big Bang theory by Georges Lemaître, dates back to 1927, but it was generally accepted only in 1964 when most scientists were convinced that experimental data confirmed that an event like the Big Bang actually took place.

Lemaître, a Belgian Catholic priest and physicist, developed the equations of the Big Bang[85] and suggested that the distancing of nebulae was due to the expansion of the cosmos, based on observations of a proportionality between distance and spectral shift (now known as Hubble's law).

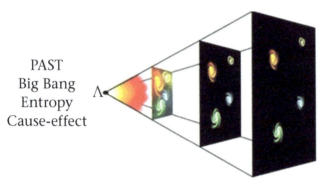

PAST
Big Bang
Entropy
Cause-effect

**Figure 19 – The Big Bang**

In 1929 Edwin Hubble and Milton Humason noted that the distance of galaxies is proportional to their *red shift*, i.e. the shift towards lower frequencies of light that usually occurs when a light source moves away from the observer or when the observer moves away from the source. The spectrum of light emitted from galaxies, quasars, or distant supernovae appears shifted to lower frequencies when compared with the spectrum of corresponding closer objects, indicating that

---

85. Lemaître, G. (1947), "Un Univers homogène de masse constante et de rayon croissant rendant compte de la vitesse radiale des nébuleuses extra-galactiques," *Annales de la Société Scientifique de Bruxelles*, vol. 47, April, p. 49.

galaxies are moving away from each other and that the Universe is in a phase of expansion. Since the distance between galaxy clusters appears to be increasing, going back in time it becomes possible to construe density and temperature becoming increasingly higher until a point is reached where their maximum values tend towards infinity and the physical laws of the forward-in-time equations are no longer valid.

In cosmology, the *Big Crunch* is a hypothesis exactly symmetrical to the Big Bang, and predicts that the universe eventually will stop expanding and begin collapsing on itself to the state where it began, and then initiate another Big Bang. In this way the universe would last forever, going through repeated phases of expansion and contraction.

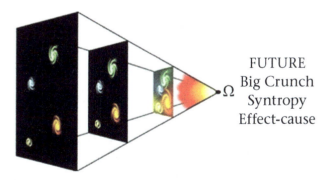

**Figure 20 – The Big Crunch**

In an attempt to explain these observations, physicists have introduced the propositions of *dark energy*, dark fluid, or phantom energy. The most important property of dark energy is that it has a negative pressure that is distributed relatively homogeneously in space, a kind of anti-gravitational force driving the galaxies apart. This mysterious anti-gravitational force is considered to be a cosmological constant that will lead the universe to expand exponentially. To this day, however, no one knows what dark energy actually is, or where it comes from.

In 2008 Professor José Senovilla, Marc Mars, and Raül Vera of the University of the Basque Country, Bilbao, and the University of Salamanca, Spain, published a paper in the journal *Physical Review*[86] in which they dismiss dark energy as fiction. The corollary of their thesis is that dark energy does not exist, but rather that time is slowing down, a process infinitesimally slow from a human perspective, but in terms of cosmology, by studying light from stars that exploded billions of years ago, it could easily be measured.

The diverging and converging process, vibrating between peaks of expansion and contraction, is another example of the entropy/syntropy exchange, in this case at the cosmic level of the universe in which the time direction is reversed.

---

86. Mars, M., Senovilla, J.M.M., and Vera, R. (2008), "Is the accelerated expansion evidence of a forthcoming change of signature on the brane?" *Physical Review D*, 77, 027501.

These two time-symmetrical movements constantly interact in the form of a continuous interplay between diverging and converging forces, causality and retrocausality, entropy and syntropy. In the Big Bang, energy and matter are governed by the positive, diverging process of entropy, while in the Big Crunch they diverge from an initial point of origin, directed by the negative converging force of syntropy,

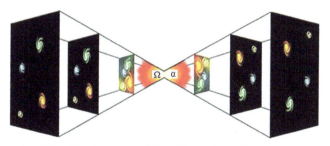

**Figure 21 – Big Bang and Big Crunch cycles**

# 24. SCIENTIFIC THEORIES

Six criteria are considered to be fundamental in the development of a scientific theory:[87]

1. *Simplicity:* a theory should embody as few "entities" as possible (this criterion is known as "Ockham's Razor").

2. It should have few, or preferably no, adjustable parameters.

3. It should be mathematically consistent.

4. It should satisfy all of the known data, including unexplained or anomalous data, or data dismissed as a "coincidence" according to previous theories.

5. It should obey causality: every effect should have a cause, whether forward or backward-in-time causality.

6. It should be falsifiable, making testable predictions.

---

87. Hotson, D.L. (2002), "Dirac's Equation and the Sea of Negative Energy," *Infinite Energy*, 43.

*Ockham's Razor* affirms that *"Entia non sunt multiplicanda praeter necessitate,"* or "Elements are not multiplied if it is not necessary to do so," and maintains that the trend of universal laws is that of economy and simplicity, with the lowest possible number of entities.

The second criterion implies that a valid scientific theory should allow for few, or preferably, no adjustable parameters, yet the prevailing Standard Model of particle physics requires at least nineteen parameters and considers only the forward-in-time solution of the fundamental equations.

Closely related to the second criterion, the third criterion requires that no equation should lead to impossible results, such as infinite values. In the Standard Model divisions that tend to infinity are common and these values need to be normalized, which means that the desired values have to be entered by hand, which would not work if we did not already know the answer. Equations thereby lose their predictive power and violate the requirement that the results of the model and empirical data should agree.

The fifth criterion states that every effect should obey causality, whether forward or backward in time. By rejecting the idea of retrocausality, the Standard Model finds it impossible to explain the causal chain that produces "anomalous" effects such as non-locality, the unified field, or entanglement. By accepting the negative-time solution, many of the mysterious properties of quantum mechanics become clear consequences of causes that act from the future. For instance, since backwards-in-time diverging energy must propagate at a speed greater than the speed of light, the information it carries can be seen to travel over infinite spaces instantaneously.

The sixth criterion requires that a scientific model should produce verifiable hypotheses. By refusing to acknowledge the negative-time solutions the Standard Model does not meet this basic criterion of a valid scientific theory.

From all this it is evident that in its present form the Standard Model of contemporary physics does not meet the prerequisites that qualify it as a scientific theory. Yet virtually all of its shortcomings in this regard could easily be resolved by incorporating the negative time-symmetric solution into its calculations. Otherwise, it, and we, will continue to be locked into an increasingly hardened mechanistic paradigm.

# 25 RELATIONAL SCIENCE

Science is a systematic enterprise that builds on and organizes knowledge in the form of empirical observations and testable predictions. In the seventeenth century, Sir Francis Bacon devised a method that allowed cause and effect relations to be studied in a replicable and objective fashion, an approach that came to be known as the *scientific method*,[88] which has led to many great scientific advancements over the ensuing centuries. But when applied to life, the scientific method displays significant shortcomings. For one thing, it can study only cause-and-effect relations, and for another, since it is based on statistics and the comparison of groups, it requires the amassing of huge accumulations of quantitative data.

Over time, science and the scientific method have come to be viewed as synonymous, which not only confounds a body of knowledge with the method used to acquire it, but also limits the boundaries of science by excluding all that is

---

88. Bacon, F. (1620). *Novum Organum, Or True Directions Concerning The Interpretation Of Nature.* Thomas Fowler (ed., notes, etc.) McMillan and Co., Clarendon Press, Oxford (1878).

syntropic, finalistic, and retrocausal. The scientific method is also susceptible to three serious errors:

1. *Extreme values.* A single extreme value, or outlier, can influence statistical calculations and lead to incorrect results.

2. *Data transformation.* When a given value is subjected to a mathematical function, calculations can vary depending on the nature of the function employed.

3. *Inappropriate hypotheses.* If an effect is observed in the direction opposite to the experiment's pre-stated hypothesis, differences cannot be assessed and the unanticipated effect must be disregarded.

#  CONCLUDING OBSERVATIONS

The implications of the extension of science to include the negative energy solution was described by Fantappiè in the following letter to a friend:

> In the days just before Christmas 1941, as a consequence of conversations with two colleagues, a physicist and a biologist, I was suddenly projected into a new panorama, which radically changed the vision of science and of the Universe which I had inherited from my teachers, and which I had always considered the strong and certain ground on which to base my scientific investigations. Suddenly I saw the possibility of interpreting a wide range of solutions (the anticipated potentials) of the wave equation which can be considered the fundamental law of the Universe. These solutions had been always rejected as impossible, but suddenly they appeared possible, and they explained a new category of phenomena which I later named syntropic, totally different from the entropic ones, of the mechanical, physical and chemical laws, which obey only the principle of

classical causation and the law of entropy. Syntropic phenomena, which are instead represented by those strange solutions of the anticipated potentials, should obey the two opposite principles of finality (moved by a final cause placed in the future, and not by a cause which is placed in the past) and differentiation, and also be non-causable in a laboratory. This last characteristic explains why this type of phenomena has never been reproduced in a laboratory, and its finalistic properties justified the refusal among scientists, who accepted without any doubt the assumption that finalism is a "metaphysical" principle, outside Science and Nature. This assumption obstructed the way to a calm investigation of the real existence of this second type of phenomena; an investigation which I accepted to carry out, even though I felt as if I were falling into an abyss, with incredible consequences and conclusions. It suddenly seemed as if the sky were falling apart, or at least the certainties on which mechanical science had based its assumptions. It appeared to me clear that these syntropic, finalistic phenomena which lead to differentiation and could not be reproduced in a laboratory, were real, and existed in nature, as I could recognize them in the living systems. The properties of this new law, opened consequences which were just incredible and which could deeply change the biological, medical, psychological, and social sciences.

The introduction of advanced waves in physics would be primarily theoretical, but in the life sciences such as biology, medicine, psychology, or sociology it would carry important pragmatic implications. These disciplines now approach pathologies, illnesses, and social crises in a causal mechanistic way, which leads, in an increasingly alarming fashion, to incorrect diagnoses, inefficiency, and increased costs.

Social and cultural milestones are marked by counter-intuitive discoveries. For example, it was once intuitive to believe the Earth flat and that the Sun revolved around the Earth. Today it is intuitive to imagine that time flows from the past to the future, but counter-intuitive to imagine that past, present and future coexist. In the paper "A novel interpretation of the Klein-Gordon equation," K. B. Wharton concludes that:

> It is obvious that quantum mechanics is counter-intuitive, but it must be counter-intuitive for a reason—some human intuition that fundamentally contradicts some physical principle. One example of this would be the well-known conflict between our direct experience of time and the more symmetric treatment of time in

fundamental physics. If the counter-intuitive aspects of quantum mechanics could be explained via classical fields symmetrically constrained by both past and future events, then it would be a mistake to reject such a solution based solely on our time-asymmetric intuitions.[89]

The change that is emerging on the horizon involves the paradigmatic shift from the mechanistic vision to the new supercausal and syntropic vision, which requires the counter-intuitive fact that time flows differently from how we perceive it in our conscious everyday experience.

While dealing with mechanistic and simple systems, the cause and effect approach is adequate. But in dealing with complex living systems retrocausal forces take a prominence as quantum forces enter into the equation of life. In human life, and in all living and self-organizing systems, both causal and retrocausal forces continuously interact.

Although much of this book has focused on the logical and pragmatic implications of the entropy/syntropy theory, perhaps the most profound aspect of it is that it introduces love into the realm

---

[89]. Wharton, K.B. (2009), "A novel interpretation of the Klein-Gordon equation," *Foundation of Physics*, 2009, 40(3): 313–332.

of modern science. Syntropy, like love, has the power to transform and unite the disparate elements in our lives. As the organizing principle of creation, evolution, and life itself, love deserves a primary role in our worldview.[90] Nobody has expressed this recognition better than Pierre Teilhard de Chardin, when he predicted that

> Someday, after we have mastered the winds, the waves, the tides and gravity, we shall harness for God the energies of love. Then for the second time in the history of the world, man will have discovered fire.[91]

---

90. Di Corpo, U. (1996). *Syntropy: The Theorem of Love,* Kindle Editions.

91. Teilhard de Chardin, P. *On Love.* NY: Harper & Row (1967), pp. 33-34.

# ABOUT THE AUTHORS

ANTONELLA VANNINI is a practicing psychotherapist and hypnotherapist with a PhD in cognitive psychology who has conducted experimental research on emotions and retrocausality. A Tai Chi instructor and expert in martial arts, Vannini is interested in the encounter between East and West. She is now exploring techniques to harmonize mind and body, as well as developing the vital needs theory and the uses of the law of syntropy in the field of psychotherapy.

ULISSE DI CORPO holds degrees in experimental psychology and a PhD in statistics and social research. He works in the field of social research and provides methodological support and software tools to researchers. In 1977 he developed the vital needs theory, which was the subject of his thesis in psychology and statistics. He is currently working on the interaction of syntropy and entropy. More information is available at www.sintropia.it.

## OTHER BOOKS BY ICRL PRESS

*Margins of Reality: The Role of Consciousness in the Physical World*
 by Robert G. Jahn and Brenda J. Dunne

*Filters and Reflections: Perspectives on Reality*
 edited by Brenda Dunne, Elissa Hoeger, Robert Jahn, and Zachary Jones

*In the Beginning: Creation Myths from Around the World*
 by Carolyn North and Adrienne Robinson

*Consciousness and the Source of Reality:
The PEAR Odyssey*
 by Robert G. Jahn and Brenda J. Dunne

*Mediumistic Phenomena: Observed in a Series of Sessions with Eusapia Palladino*
 by Filippo Bottazzi, translated by Antonio Giuditta and Irmeli Routti

*Quirks of the Quantum Mind*
 by Robert G. Jahn and Brenda J. Dunne

*Manifestations of Mind in Matter: Conversations about Art, Science, and Spirit*
 by Iebele Abel

*The Spirit of Spinoza: Healing the Mind*
 by Neal Grossman

*Bava's Gift: Awakening to the Impossible*
 by Michael Urheber

---

Available in print and digital formats from Amazon and other retailers. For more information see http://icrl.org/icrl-press.

---